"Here is a tender and helpful book with a pastor[...] her readers the essential elements of attachme[...] them partner with God for their healing. Thi[...] read it."

Lore Ferguson Wilbert, author of *The Understory* (forthcoming),
A Curious Faith, and *Handle with Care*

"As followers of Jesus, we know that He promises to be with us always. Yet, either out of personal hurts, distractions, or ignorance, we do not realize the power, balm, and consistency of God's presence with us. Summer Gross opens one's eyes with insight and practical help to know Emmanuel—God-with-us—in all aspects of one's life."

Foley Beach, Archbishop and Primate, Anglican Church in North America

"*The Emmanuel Promise* blends centuries of spiritual practices with the science of attachment. Everyone can improve their attachment and interactions with God, but can we maintain awareness when life is busy or bumpy? *The Emmanuel Promise* provides us with stories and simple practices for building secure relational spirituality. Your brain, heart, and friends will be glad you did."

Rev. Jim Wilder, PhD, chief neurotheologian of Life Model Works
and coauthor of *Escaping Enemy Mode*

"Many of us can sing the words, but we struggle to believe them: 'Jesus loves me, this I know, for the Bible tells me so.' We long to live in assurance of that good news, but it feels too good to be true. In sharing her own story as well as wisdom she's gained from years as a spiritual director, Summer Joy Gross offers both a compelling diagnosis for our spiritual disorder and a gentle but firm path toward healing. This is a book I wish I'd had years ago."

Richella J. Parham, author of *Mythical Me* and *A Spiritual Formation Primer* and board chair of Renovaré

"Summer Joy Gross recognizes that the deepest ache of the human heart is to find a safe place of belonging and non-comparing love. Through *The Emmanuel Promise*, Summer takes us by the hand and gently leads us to the sacred space of divine security and soul rest, integrating cutting-edge insights on attachment theory with the ancient art of spiritual direction. Summer provides the reader with a much-needed, Spirit-filled guide that draws them into intimacy with God. *The Emmanuel Promise* is a treasure trove of insight, inspiration, and practical application, desperately needed at this precise moment."

Terry Wardle, author of *Healing Care, Healing Prayer*
and founder of Healing Care Ministries

"We've been told God is a loving parent, but do we feel deep down that this is true? If you're nodding, but your heart isn't entirely sure, this powerful book is for you. Only a few chapters in, I could hear with much more clarity the tender voice of Emmanuel saying, "Welcome home." A book like *The Emmanuel Promise* does not come along very often. Here a talented writer with a depth of wisdom and experience helps us both diagnose our wounds and pursue healing practices. Do not miss this excellent book."

Christie Purifoy, author of *Placemaker* and *Seedtime and Harvest*

"*Love* and *presence*. Two important words so easily underestimated. But, oh, the depth and necessity of this pair. In her book, *The Emmanuel Promise*, Summer Joy Gross acts as a nurturing guide, as she helps us make our way to the transformative dynamics of presence, attachment, and God's love. Be seen by Summer's own 'safe pair of eyes' as she draws you to the table of the Beloved. Grow in your awareness of the nearness of God's love and make your way to the connection you long for. Summer is a caring and trustworthy guide in matters of the soul."

Gem Fadling, founder of Unhurried Living
and author of *Hold That Thought*

"While many us know information about God, read the Bible, and pray, we can often feel a disconnect between what we believe, how we live, and what we experience of God. Summer Gross reminds weary believers that God's nearness—in the language of attunement and attachment—can be known through practices of resilient hope in a worn-out world. Rather than simply providing us with more information, Gross leads us back to attachment with God through prayers and practices, showing us that it's never too late to grow in wholeness."

Ashley Hales, director of research at the Willowbrae Institute
and author of *A Spacious Life*

"*The Emmanuel Promise* is a book you'll want to read slowly—not because it's difficult to understand but because it's deep, layered, and confronting in healthy, meaningful ways. Summer Joy Gross manages to combine the wisdom of Scripture and church mothers and fathers with current, evidence-based research on attachment theory in order to help us better understand ourselves, our relationships, and how we perceive and connect with God. It is not a book for consumption but for prayerful and thoughtful application. *The Emmanuel Promise* is a gift for those in search of a gentle, experienced guide on their journey of spiritual formation."

Adriel Booker, author of *Grace Like Scarlett*
and *Tethered to Hope* (forthcoming)

THE EMMANUEL PROMISE

THE
EMMANUEL PROMISE

DISCOVERING THE SECURITY
OF A LIFE HELD BY GOD

SUMMER JOY GROSS

BakerBooks

a division of Baker Publishing Group
Grand Rapids, Michigan

Published by Baker Books
a division of Baker Publishing Group
Grand Rapids, Michigan
BakerBooks.com

Printed in the United States of America

Library of Congress Cataloging-in-Publication Data
Names: Gross, Summer Joy, 1975– author.
Title: The emmanuel promise : discovering the security of a life held by God / Summer Joy Gross.
Description: Grand Rapids, Michigan : Baker Books, a division of Baker Publishing Group, [2024] | Includes bibliographical references.
Identifiers: LCCN 2023036740 | ISBN 9781540903662 (paper) | ISBN 9781540903884 (cloth) | ISBN 9781493444106 (ebook)
Subjects: LCSH: Christian life. | Spirituality—Christianity. | Neurosciences. | Attachment behavior.
Classification: LCC BV4501.3 .G7656 2024 | DDC 248.2—dc23/eng/20231122
LC record available at https://lccn.loc.gov/2023036740

The author is represented by the literary agency of Mary DeMuth Literary.

Baker Publishing Group publications use paper produced from sustainable forestry practices and postconsumer waste whenever possible.

24   25   26   27   28   29   30   7   6   5   4   3   2   1

To my mother, whose passion for this topic has informed every chapter. To my father, who had tears after listening to me read these words and tenderly held my hand as we walked around the block. I'm so grateful for the privilege of being your daughter.

CONTENTS

Introduction

His Face Turned toward You

Transitions can sometimes reveal the potholes of our internal world. Sometimes they create them. But stories wired into our brains in adolescence can become hard to wire out. In adolescence, our brains are porous, moldable.[1] My story may not be a story of abandonment or the death of a parent, but it's my story, the story of a young girl's vulnerability and four years of loneliness and hypervigilance, four years of "little t" trauma.

Not all stories of trauma have a shock factor. Some are slow, a twisting and wringing out over several years' time—in this case, four. Therapists talk about "big T" traumas and "little t" traumas. "Big T" traumas are events: a death of a loved one, a rape, a divorce. "Little t" traumas signal an internal bruise, a repetition of hurt, a lie compounded, an atmosphere of shame, all unseen ticks on the page of an autobiography, but still tender.

Both types of trauma create the neural pathways, roadways in our brain, that all other relationships travel down. This formation of neural pathways begins in the first three years of our lives as the quality of our attachment with our first caregiver is established. And this is what I want you to hear. Every experience we have with our main caregiver creates expectations for future care. In fact, it sets up our expectations for care for all our relationships going forward, even our relationship with God. Traumas of all kinds can rip and tear at a secure attachment, leaving a new story in its place, a story ruled by shame, fear, and rejection.

When I was ten, my family made a simple cross-country move, a common occurrence in many families. We stuffed the U-Haul, drove sixteen hours from the rugged rocks of the southern Maine coast where my dad had been a surgical resident, and unpacked in the flat cornfields of northern Ohio. My dad was going back to his roots. His ancestors had been given land in Huron County as a part of the Firelands, which was an act of Connecticut legislature. After the British had burned their town during the Revolutionary War, his family was given 168 acres to farm. Centuries later, we were retracing their route from New England back to that same county in Ohio.

In moving back home, Dad was keeping a promise to a doctor who had funded his first year in medical school in Italy. He had asked Dad to return to provide care for their small-town hospital. Dr. Kauffman had passed away, but Dad believed promises were made to be kept.

Since then, I've learned how traumatic a move like this is in the life of an adolescent. Research shows that "moving is the third most stressful event, after the death of a loved one and divorce."[2]

Before the move, each day of fourth grade, my teacher in Portland passed out black-and-white mottled composition notebooks and set an egg timer for thirty minutes of delicious silence. The only rule? We had to keep our pencil tip on the paper. I used the page to lament and whine, to process and adventure. I learned to play on the page. I learned to pray on the page.

On the first day of fifth grade, I pushed through the large metal door of my new private school in Celeryville, Ohio, a farm village lined with basketball hoops. I was sporting baggy plaid overalls, a clipped Maine accent, and an awkward smile. I said things like "wicked good" and "aunt," not "ant." That first day, I was called a clown, made fun of for my accent, and informed that my high-tops were so very last year. (Please read that last line in the accent of a Valley Girl while flipping your permed ponytail over your shoulder.) When I got home that afternoon, I hid the overalls in the bottom of my toy chest along with any hope of an easy adjustment.

I was an Anne of Green Gables in a Hoosiers world.

I was bullied, one small dig at a time, and where other children may have been able to laugh it off and launch it back, I had no such shield, no such skill. Recesses were spent on the volleyball court with the clichéd picking of sides. Do I hear you groaning? Put a hundred junior highers in a room, and fifth-grade me would have won at the game of awkward. The ball stung when it slapped the tender insides of my arms, and I rubbed the sting. The looks and eye rolls stung too, but I never learned to rub their tenderness away.

These were tall, farm-grown people. Their Dutch grandparents had ingeniously drained acres of swamp and discovered some of the most fertile land in America. They called it The Muck. They were smart, entrepreneurial farmers. My classmates worked the fields in the summers, pulling green onions beside migrant workers from Mexico. They worked long hours in the sun and came back in the fall with a dark tan and a new vocabulary they were dying to try out.

The houses in the village were lined with basketball nets, and dads came home in the evening to play H-O-R-S-E with their kids. Three of the girls in my class reached six feet tall in the sixth grade and mastered the effortless layup. They had the gift of a village. Aunts. Uncles. Cousins. They were surrounded by group identity, a shared story, a common mission. They had never before known the anxiety of being uprooted.

Now, as a mom, I see that farming village in a completely different light. It's exactly the type of place I would have wanted to raise my own kids. Open doors. Safe families. Dads who drove their white pickup trucks to the nearby fields. Moms who made peanut butter and jelly sandwiches on the kitchen counter for the kids to grab on summer afternoons. On Sunday mornings, inside the red-brick Christian Reformed church across from the school, families sat down in familiar pews. Sunlight streamed through long windows and bounced off white wood. Moms pulled square mints out of their purses before the sermon was preached. The children were known and embraced by a generous childhood.

But what's paradise for one person can be torment for another. Perhaps I was like the little matchstick girl, always looking in the windows at a continual feast but never invited to take a seat at the table.

When my family and I drove west, our own strong, Maine roots tore. For five years, we had gathered at Jerry and Mary Goodall's house on Sunday nights for small group Bible study. This group held us together in their generous arms as Dad spent hundred-hour workweeks at the hospital training. We held hands as we sang the doxology in four parts, voices bouncing off the slate floor in the entryway. Casserole dishes, plates of cucumbers from the garden, traditional brown bread, and B&M baked beans with hot dogs circled the table. All the kids walked in and out of the teachings and the kitchen snacking on spice cookies and drinking milk from small Tupperware cups. I sat in Mom's lap as we learned about the Psalms or I sprawled across the floor, napping on a couch pillow while the guitar was strummed. Now, here I was, sixteen hours away in Ohio, wondering where my village was.

Every morning before school, I slid open the minivan door and walked into the small Christian school in Celeryville, and I wondered how to stay small enough to survive until 2:45 p.m. Hour by hour, I stayed on a seesaw of fight-or-flight. Every night I strategized how I would build bridges. Maybe I could compliment a girl on her new shirt from the Limited. I would pray for a smile, pray for friendship. I contemplated bringing extra chocolate chip cookies in my lunch to hand out. "Nice" became my coping mechanism, my strategy, and my surprise attack, but the connection never lasted long. I tried to comprehend this new culture and the language, the facial expressions, the mannerisms, the elbows slammed on the table, the huffing, the eye-rolling. After four years of this, hypervigilance was carved into my nervous system.

We all need a safe pair of eyes to land on when we're moving into fight-or-flight. We regulate our emotions through glances of kindness. We look for someone who knows us, someone who carries the truth of our value, someone who holds us in friendship when we're in a swirl of anxiety. Each day I walked in alone, a thousand nerve endings awake on my skin. For four years, I lived without the safety of a kind pair of eyes.

The Still Face

Our brains need *attunement* like they need nourishment. We need someone to mirror our hurt back to us and say, "Ouch. I see your pain and I'm not going anywhere." Attunement occurs when one person reads or tunes into the inner world of the other person with understanding and support. This is vital, especially for children. Why? A child is not able to regulate their emotions on their own. Their caregiver provides the empathetic presence the child needs to begin to make sense of their fear when awakening from a nightmare. Their pain is rightsized only when the child gives it voice and then experiences the empathy in their caregiver's eyes.

When a child feels seen and understood by a caregiver, they feel safe enough to metabolize the emotion. Without attunement, the child either revs up their emotion to a higher degree or they begin the process of numbing because the emotion is too much to handle on their own. With attunement from their caregiver, the child eventually learns to internalize the caregiver's compassion, to self-regulate, and to use the caregiver's brain as the first map of their own emotions. Neuroscientist Dr. Daniel Siegel uses four S's to describe what we need to feel when we are reaching out for attunement: safe, seen, soothed, and secure.[3]

Years after our move to Ohio, I recognized the same disintegration I experienced walking through those metal doors while watching a video of Harvard professor Ed Tronick's Still Face experiment.[4] Tronick's research into attachment, which revealed the quality of the bond between child and caregiver, helped further our understanding of attachment theory. The more secure the bond, the more the child was able to grow up moving about in the world with a sense of safety, wonder, and ease.

In the video, a mom mirrored her one-year-old daughter's laughter and curiosity and attuned to her emotions. When the little girl pointed, the mom looked and laughed with obvious delight. When she reached for the mother from her seat in a high chair, the mom laced their fingers together. The mom was attuning, constantly reading the signals, the emotions, and the needs of her daughter. Next, at Dr. Tronick's instruction, the mother turned her face away and stripped all emotion from her expression. When she turned back toward her daughter, she showed a face devoid of any hint of awareness or connection called Still Face.

But Still Face is not neutral.[5]

In the video, the young girl made facial expressions expecting her mother to respond. She tried to grab her mother's attention by pointing playfully, laughing, and engaging. Finally, after two minutes, the infant's shock turned to confusion and then grief and anger and, finally, total emotional mayhem. She went limp. She would have slidden onto the floor if she hadn't been firmly clicked into the high chair. Finally, she screeched and banged on the tray. The emotional stress caused her to fold in on herself.

Can you feel that in your gut? The search for a face engaged? I sure can. It's one of our greatest needs and the source of our greatest fear: the shame of everyone turning away. We fear being alone in a crowd because every face around us has become Still Face.

But here's my question: how many of us experience God as Still Face? How often do we believe He's emotionally unavailable in the middle of our being tossed by great waves, that we have to yell, repeat our needs ad nauseum, find the right words that will act as an incantation, or prove our worthiness?

Do you think that's how the disciples felt in Luke 8:22–25 when a storm started tossing their boat like a plastic vessel in a toddler's bathtub and Jesus was sound asleep? He was exhausted from days of teaching on the mountain, healing Peter's mother-in-law, and tending to the townspeople's abundant needs pressing in all around Him. I can imagine that being on the open lake with a few safe people sounded like just the sort of peace Jesus was looking for after compassion had wearied His body. I wonder if "Where is your faith?" was more like "Do you still not know me? Do you not believe that I will never leave you helpless?"

Our greatest fear is being abandoned, that God will be absent or asleep when we need Him most. Our deepest *need*, then, becomes a question: Will I be safe, seen, soothed, and secure when life has me flat on the floor? Over and over throughout Scripture, God's response is "I am with you," embodied in Emmanuel. God-with-us is not just a tagline. It is God Himself with us in the mess and mire of our lives. God-with-us is the promise of an available and attuned Divine Caregiver, turned toward us, His ear open to our every cry, not from afar, but right here in the room. Divine Love, then, is not ephemeral, here today and gone tomorrow. It is the solid promise of a face always shining toward us. The invitation of this book—and, of course, of our lifetime—is to become awake and aware of Love always reaching out.

A Face like the Sunrise

Let's pause for a moment to connect this to our own stories. When you walked into the room as a child, how did your dad greet you? Imagine your dad after work, sitting in the corner on his laptop or behind a stack of paperwork on his desk. Now, you peek around the corner and yell, "Daddy!" What happens? What does his face look like? Do you come in and jump onto his lap? Do you keep your distance? Do you wonder if he heard you? Does he scowl? Does he put his index finger up, letting you know he doesn't have time right now?

Now imagine walking into a room where God is "at work." What happens? Does He put out His hand and ask you to wait because He's busy? Or does His face light up as He holds out His arms and welcomes you with eagerness?

Next, visualize walking toward God the Father with the brokenness of your sin in your arms, the aftermath of your rage still knotted in your stomach, your computer with pornography still open, Jack Daniels still on your breath, your words slurring as you stumble forward. Tell me what His face looks like now.

The prodigal son was expecting full-on wrath. He had humiliated his dad, asking for his inheritance even before his father's death, and now he was crawling back home hungry after gambling away his dad's legacy in a Middle Eastern Vegas. He could no longer afford even a 4 for $4 from Wendy's. He got a job at a pig farm and spent his days smelling like pig slop as he considered sharing their food and lay down to sleep. In complete desperation, the prodigal limped home, remembering his dad's servants didn't have to root through the trash for supper. As he got closer, he rehearsed what he was going to say, fully expecting to hear an "I told you so" or "get out of my sight." He expected Still Face, but instead, his father's face looked like a sunrise. Full of complete and utter joy. Nothing but welcome. Before the son could even repent, his father threw a coat over his son's dirty jeans and T-shirt and phoned home for steaks to be put on the grill.

He was expecting wrath from his father. Maybe you were too. Maybe he was expecting a dressing down ending with a slammed door. Maybe you were expecting an icy presence, hands on hips with eyebrows raised and the word "Again?" thrown in your direction.

Maybe you were just expecting disinterest. God's attention is limited, right? He doesn't have the ability to look up every time you walk into the room. Deep down you believe He's busy elsewhere, somewhere more important.

All of this is what a spiritual director calls "helpful information," but don't worry, you're not being graded. Knowing more about our expectations around discipline and care helps us learn more about what we expect in our experience of God.[6]

Attachment with God

Every Tuesday during the summer before I went to college, I walked through the door to Trudy's office in a repurposed, white clapboard house in Norwalk, Ohio, and sat down. Trudy, a marriage and family therapist, had been trained at nearby Ashland Seminary to pray her Christian clients through trauma. She taught me to go from a sense of safety—in my case, a couch in our family room—to a memory, then watch it unfold in front of me and ask God, Where are You in the room? How do You feel about what happened to me? Slowly, memories were being transformed as I watched Jesus weep with me.

As I prayed with Trudy, I remembered pushing open that large metal door to my junior high. But this time, Jesus walked into my fifth-grade classroom, set up a cross, and got up on it. I was stunned. Silenced. Christ on the cross took my breath away. There was nothing more that needed to be said.

I couldn't put this prayer experience into words for a long time, but every time I thought of the school building, or even dreamed of it, the cross was there in the fifth-grade room. Every time I saw myself pushing through those doors, I was going to visit Jesus, and He was declaring, "This place is mine. I hold the power here." The tree of life had been planted. The roots were spreading the kingdom through my memories.

Somehow, this message also endowed me with value. I heard Him say, "She's mine. I died for this one." Encountering Christ's presence in this place of hurt transformed my junior high experience from one of shame to one of safety and security. If I walked into any of the rooms in the school in my memory, the power of the cross completely shifted my emotions in the present. I was secure. Emmanuel present was the only message I needed; He was the final Word.

My internal earthquake ended in His presence.

Emmanuel Is in the Room

Years later, at the Advanced Formational Prayer Conference in Ashland, Ohio, I sat at a round table facing Dr. Anne Halley, a spiritual director, professor, and practitioner in this realm of attachment with God.[7] The fluorescent lights were strong, but the autumn light pouring in through the windows of the conference room was even stronger. That day, Anne wore a blue sweater and her characteristic warm smile. It was 2010. Anne was teaching us how becoming aware of our attachment with our first caregiver still affects our relationship with God. During our session, she invited us to ask the question, "Jesus, where are You in the room on my behalf?"

I sensed Jesus was far away in the corner but near in His attentiveness. He was turning toward each of us in delight. In fact, He was turning toward *me* in delight. I was experiencing the Emmanuel—God-*with*-us—holding my gaze with tenderness. The room stopped spinning. My breath deepened. My shoulders dropped. In the midst of a full conference room, my orientation shifted from overwhelmed to grounded. *Christ is here*, I thought. *He who holds the world in the palm of His hand is present.* As I opened up my awareness to the Emmanuel's presence, I experienced feeling safe, seen, soothed, and secure.

What if we could experience an attachment with God so grounding that we feel safe in every room because we are oriented to His anchoring presence? What if we learn to stop at every threshold, take a deep breath, and ask, "Jesus, where are You in *this* room?" And then as we step into the space, we join the One who is perpetually welcoming His children.

That day, I began to comprehend what the disciples learned that stormy night on the Sea of Galilee: peace is a person, and when we are aware of His presence, waves of anxiety are stilled. I also learned that coming awake to this truth is our chief work.

Author C. S. Lewis said, "We may ignore, but we can nowhere evade, the presence of God. The world is crowded with Him. He walks everywhere *incognito*. And the *incognito* is not always hard to penetrate. The real labour is to attend. In fact, to come awake. Still more, to remain awake."[8]

Brother Lawrence of the Resurrection, the author of the letters that became the classic text *The Practice of the Presence of God*, said, "I cannot understand how religious people can live contented lives without the practice of the presence of God. For myself, I withdraw as much as I can to the deepest recesses of my soul with Him, and while I am thus with Him I fear nothing; but the least turning away from Him is hell for me."[9]

Then Brother Lawrence invited us to form this habit: "In the beginning a persistent effort is needed to form the habit of continually talking with God and to refer all we do to Him but that after a little care, His love brings us to it without any difficulty."[10]

Over the last decade and a half, I've asked myself this question daily: How would my anxiety today shift if I awakened to God's presence, the promise of Emmanuel? What if I could be safe, seen, soothed, and secure because Jesus's face was always shining toward me, always attentive, always connected? Like a dancer doing pirouettes while focused on a clock in the back of an auditorium, could I orient myself to the presence of my Emmanuel, eyes trained on the One who is always attentive to me? Psychologists who study attachment theory have described *secure attachment* as a bond between child and caregiver where there is trust that care is available. So I began to wonder if I could experience the building of a secure attachment to the almighty God.

Dotted throughout the Old and New Testaments, the presence of God was provided as the security of God's people, for their safety, for their peace, for their comfort, and for the ultimate encouragement that the God of the universe walked right beside them.

Throughout the Gospels, we see that, in the presence of Jesus, stories are transformed, people are fed, the dead are raised, storms still, and darkness flees. Rooms shift when we become oriented to the presence of Christ.

But here's the question we must ask if we seek a secure attachment with God: Has this concept of Emmanuel become so overfamiliar that it has become lodged in our logical left brain and is never given the capacity to form the basis of our security in the world? Said another way, Have we kept the promise of Emmanuel at a distance because of its familiarity?

What if you were hearing the following Scriptures for the first time?

> So do not fear, for I am with you;
>> do not be dismayed, for I am your God.
> I will strengthen you and help you;
>> I will uphold you with my righteous right hand. (Isa. 41:10)

> Have I not commanded you? Be strong and courageous. Do not be afraid; do not be discouraged, for the LORD your God *will be with you* wherever you go. (Josh. 1:9, emphasis added)

Then, there's the very last words the Emmanuel spoke before He ascended into heaven: "Surely I am with you always, to the very end of the age" (Matt. 28:20). Add to these a thousand other invitations throughout Scripture of God inviting us to walk with Him, to grab hold of His hand, and to look in His face.

Somewhere along the line we've got to ask ourselves, Did He mean what He said or was it just an inane comfort He was throwing our way before escaping into heavenly realms?

David the psalmist didn't think so. In Psalm 16:8, he wrote,

> I have set the LORD continually before me;
> Because he is at my right hand, I will not be shaken. (NASB)

David's strength was built on practicing God's presence.

How do we remain awake to the presence of God? How do we orient our lives to the promise of Emmanuel, the living Christ, walking beside us?

Discovering the answers to these two questions is the journey between these two covers. It's also the journey between birth and death. Lace up your hiking boots. Pick up your walking stick. I'll walk beside you.

But first, a few practical steps as we start down the trail together.

1. Access companion videos for each chapter at summerjoy gross.com/the-emmanuel-promise. I'll walk you through prayer experiences using the Scriptures and Monday-Morning Practicals and make everything as accessible as possible. All you have to do is push play.

2. Remember, God is the initiator. We'll talk a good bit about this later. He knocks. We open.

3. Lean on Him. One of the most important prayers I've learned to pray is this: *God, I don't have desire for You in my-self. Would You give me desire for You?* This keeps us from staying stuck in messages crafted by shame. He is the giver of every good and perfect gift, even the desire to grow.

4. Keep your pace slow. You're not going to be graded. People grow best at the pace of relationship.

5. Find your people. Don't think you have to do this work alone. Maybe you have a group already set up for this sort of journey. Read the book together. Or you can join the Presence Project[11] community and we'll walk together.

Heaven is crammed with those who have come awake to God's presence and turned toward the Son as if warming themselves after a fierce New England winter. They are wrapped. Held. Embraced.

We are living here on earth with the smallest viewpoint of the divine, filled with incessantly chattering ego needs, obsessed with safety, and carrying the heaviness of a broken world on our shoulders. This awakening to the nearness of Emmanuel is a leaning in, a learning, a listening to one whispered invitation after another.

Earth is filled with the footprints of those who have passed before us, yawning, stretching, emerging from the slumber of life to walk with our Emmanuel. The line stretches out before us: Paul, Saint Patrick, Teresa of Ávila, Saint John of the Cross, Brother Lawrence, C. S. Lewis, and on and on.

Throughout this book, we'll join them in the journey, listening as the Spirit whispers, "Come awake, come awake, come and rise up from your sleep."

———

You don't have to go it alone. For this chapter, access an Ignatian Imaginative Prayer of Jesus blessing the children that you can do alone (as often as you'd like) or share it with a group. Find the video at summerjoygross.com/the-emmanuel-promise.

PART I

INSECURE ATTACHMENT

Anxious for Emmanuel

1

Your First Attachment Stories

The concept of adoption is liberally sprinkled throughout the Old and New Testaments. With reason. We have a new Abba, a covenant relationship bought by blood through the work of the cross and enacted through baptism, but the road to a bond with our new Abba is rocky. Why? Don't miss this. *We bring attachment wounds from our original bond with our first caregiver into our relationship with God.*

Why do we struggle to receive the love of our new heavenly Father? We are daughters and sons of the Most High, yet we search high and low for love, for worth, and for provision. We sit outside the kingdom holding a little tin cup, while the King's arms are always open. We keep foraging in old locations where we used to find our needs met.

Just like an adoptee, we too need thousands of felt experiences of care to believe that adoption is more than just a formal assent; it's a constant invitation. We need thousands of experiences of attunement and comfort, peace and connection, before our first reaction to pain is to run home to our Father's arms. We must grow into love.

Attachment Wounds

We do not come to our relationship with God empty and open, a tabula rasa. The slate of our neural pathways is not wiped clean when we pass through the baptismal waters. Scripture was not our first teacher and Sunday school lessons were merely building on previously acquired information.

First, we have to wake to the messages already engraved in our brains.[1] We have preconceived ideas of what love looks like based on thousands of sensory experiences with our caregivers of love given or love withheld. These became deep, trenchlike neural pathways all other thoughts slid into.

Most of us have *attachment wounds*, twisted souvenirs from childhood, which created an insecure attachment that shapes our ability to give and receive love. We may have memorized Scriptures that gave us the correct information, but long before we could grasp the answers, the answers had grasped us. The story of love had already been written. For good or for ill, we lug our attachment wounds into every relationship we enter, even our relationship with God.

Many of us have been Christians for decades, ticking all the boxes. Slowly we've downgraded our expectations. When we became a Christian, we were told we would be whisked into a relationship, an adventure, a great love story. Now, after decades of serving, we're tired. Connection feels frayed at best and absent at worst. We fear that we've been adopted and abandoned, like the disciples must have felt watching Jesus ascend through the clouds. We fear His promise, "I will be with you always," was just a nicety, a spiritual promise not a felt reality. We came into this relationship wanting *more*. Not to be loved and left. Some of us already knew that story and were hoping to sign up for a different one.

The Upside-Down Triangle

It was week two of the Healing Care Group, a curriculum that invites people to experience God's healing in places of deep wounding.[2] As the members shuffled in after work, I invited them to ladle themselves a bowl of soup and grab a yeast roll still hot from the oven. In the warmth of companionship, they began to shift from worn and weary to ready to connect. I can't imagine how hard it must have been to drive home and drop off their things only to put their coat back on and drive to the church. Taking their seats, they greeted each other. They said "Good evening" and "How is your week going?" but unless they had a previous friendship, they were a little bit stiff and kept their heads forward in their bowls. All that would change in a few weeks. Each of the twelve times I've led this curriculum, people tell me they've never experienced the loving power of the body of Christ as they did during these groups. "Oh," they say, "this is what the church is supposed to feel like."

It's partly because of the size of the groups. You just can't be vulnerable or feel supported in groups over about eight.

Over time, I've also learned to create intentional safety for their vulnerability. At the start of each meeting, I make sure to remind each member that we don't "fix" or advise. This is shocking to those who are used to discipleship being more like a download than a relationship, but I remind them that the Holy Spirit is good at His job. The Spirit and the curriculum will lead us. I also know that I create the temperature for vulnerability. Whether we're confessing or lamenting, I go first. My story creates room for their story.

But all that comes in time.

When they finish their soup, I tell them to draw an upside-down triangle. I keep instructing them: "Under the bottom point, write *Me*. At the top right point, write *Mom*, and at the top left point, write *Dad*. In the line from Mom to Dad, write what their love looked like. How did Dad treat Mom? How did Mom treat Dad? Then up and down the right and left lines, write how Dad treated you and how Mom treated you. What was the quality of that love? That bond? The good, the bad, and the ugly." Then I give them a half hour to sit and reflect.

Once that time has passed, I encourage them to make their fingers into a triangle on top of the lines and slowly lift it above their head, looking through this triangle at the sky. "Most of the time," I tell them, "we view God's love through this old, old story."

THE QUALITY OF YOUR BONDS

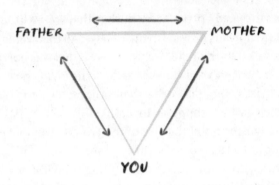

What's Your View of God?

My mom and dad were just twenty-two when I was born. I came on the scene just eighteen months after their college graduation, a January wedding (in powder blue suits), and a desperate move to Italy for medical school. They were part of the postwar baby boom, and Dad had to get scrappy to follow his dream to serve others through the medical profession. I couldn't be prouder of them. I can't imagine the courage Mom had to conjure up to give birth in a hospital full of doctors screaming Italian phrases faster than she could understand. Dad had to learn Italian well enough to take oral exams every year in an amphitheater filled with his colleagues.

I arrived into a life full of big questions, including how to pay for next week's groceries. Six months after I was born, Mom began teaching in an international school, and Dad went back to his books, translating them from Italian to English before trying to digest their contents. He took me on long walks next to the Mediterranean before I fell asleep for my morning nap and he could open his textbook again. They never made me feel like I was unwanted or a chore.

I'm so grateful for that, but early on, I believed I had to make their life as smooth as possible. Who had time for a baby's cries? Who had time for the terrible twos? I became a people pleaser, reading the room before I dared share a need. I believed love depended on perfect timing.

This, of course, transferred to my relationship with God. Many of us believe God's love is conditional, based on our performance. Because of our attachment wound, we can't imagine Love is always waiting at the road of our lives, delighted to see us, ready to throw a coat over our shoulders and welcome us home.

When I asked several Presence Project members what their view of God was growing up, and how it shifted, I received almost a hundred answers. Here are just a few:

- "Removed, disappointed, neglectful. Through very dark times and therapy and spiritual formation, it has shifted dramatically."
- "A distant benefactor, now my best friend."
- "A grumpy father. Now a kind and loving father, and also a majestic King."
- "My image of God was the same image I had of my earthly dad—busy, absent, uninterested, thought I was a burden."
- "A cosmic policeman or helicopter parent who wanted to make sure I did everything right. Judgmental gatekeeper."
- "My image of God mimicked my early father. Harsh, chaotic, ready to find fault and punish."
- "He was a God, more or less, with a hammer, ready to strike if I made a wrong move."
- "Standoffish, waiting for me to follow the prescribed rules so that He could finally use me and, 'bless her heart,' she just couldn't get it right. I have come to understand that that is not the real God. He is delighted in me and wants me to experience Him and know His love for me."

Attachment Theory 101

Attachment theory was first developed by Dr. John Bowlby, a baronet in upper-class Britain. Think *Downton Abbey* and starched, professional nannies. Bowlby was number four of six running about the nursery. He was given one hour a day with his mother after teatime and only one hour a week on Sunday afternoon with his father, who was part of the king's medical staff. Like many of that time period, Bowlby's parents believed affection would spoil their kids. Complete separation was a normal part of his family life. His mother often traveled to be with her husband, leaving the children in the nursery with only the nannies for care. In some ways, he was lucky. From infancy to age four, he had a nursemaid named Minnie who delighted in her little charge, but when he reached age four, Minnie was dismissed, and he grieved her as if he had lost a mother. After Minnie was dismissed, he was left with a sarcastic woman, Nanny Friend, who kept Bowlby and his siblings at arm's length.[3] At age seven, he was sent to a boarding school, a place that he later said he wouldn't send a dog he liked.

After Cambridge, medical school, and further psychiatric training, Bowlby worked at Priory Gates, a home for maladjusted children, and later at Canonbury where he began to notice a pattern of how many of the juvenile criminals were separated from caregivers before the age of five. During World War II he continued in this same line of study, researching children who were evacuated from London or placed in group homes so their moms could strengthen the war effort. He began to write research papers, eventually changing the mind of hospitals that demanded children be dropped off for medical care alone.

Humans are the only mammals who are dependent on our caregivers for so long. We come into the world rooting, but we're unable to find food if left to ourselves.

Every time our first caregiver came when we cried, we developed an expectation for future care.[4] Trust is an embodied experience;

it is not an assertion toward information. Trust is developed by thousands of interactions, one after another. Every time we were emotionally left stranded as children, a story was written into our neural pathways.[5] Every time we heard the sound of impatience and frustration, our brains took note. Our caregiver was completely responsible for the strength of our bond and attachment.

Another psychologist named Mary Ainsworth joined Bowlby's research team. She studied mothers with their children from infancy to thirty months and began noticing different attachment styles in the quality of the bond between parent and child. She used a research strategy she called the Strange Situation, which has been recreated over and over throughout the decades, in different geographies and with different social strata, each time with similar results.

Picture this: A mother and child enter an observation room. The child explores, plays with age-appropriate toys, and generally gets comfortable in the room while Mom observes. Then, a stranger enters and focuses attention on the child while Mom leaves for a few minutes.

This separation reveals much. How does the child behave after she or he realizes Mom has left?

When Mom comes back into the room, how the child experiences the mother's comfort is observed carefully. Then Mom walks out the door again, along with the stranger, and the child is left completely alone in the room. Finally, the stranger comes back and tries to connect with the child after which Mom returns and picks up the child to comfort her or him.

A lot of information about the child-parent bond can be gained throughout this experience. As they watch, researchers ask questions like:

How much independent play does the child engage in?

How does the child react to Mom's leaving?

How does the child react to the stranger?

Is the child able to receive Mom's comfort?

33

After the results are assessed, the child's bond or attachment is placed in one of four categories:

Insecure anxious: The child is clingy, perhaps anticipating the caregiver's absence. The child uses people-pleasing behaviors to try to keep the caregiver engaged and in the room. The child cries when the caregiver leaves and keeps crying inconsolably when they come back.

Insecure avoidant: When the caregiver returns, the child stays busy with toys, showing no visible need for the caregiver, though they may follow the caregiver out of the corner of their eyes. It's possible in most cases that the child has lost the belief that the caregiver will meet their needs. They may not believe comfort is available.

Insecure disorganized: The child is in deep distress. They wonder, *Should I go toward my caregiver? Should I move away?* The main characteristic in this child's behavior is fear of the caregiver. In many cases, this child has experienced some type of abuse. Other times, the child may feel the caregiver is bizarre and inconsistent, which could be due to a mental illness.

Secure: The child's caregiver is their secure or home base. They can play with curiosity when their caregiver is present but will be distraught when they leave the room. The caregiver easily attunes to the child, taking the child's inner temperature and reading what care is needed. The caregiver is available for co-regulation and can bring the child's emotional state back to peace.

Let's think together about your attachment (or lack of) with your own caregivers. Imagine yourself as a small child in your house. Try to answer these questions as best you can:

When you ran to your mother, were you met with comfort and emotional regulation?

What happened when you ran to your father? Was care given
generously or was it stingy?

Did you have to earn love or was it unconditional?

How were you taken care of when you were sick?

Notice your memories. Notice your feelings. How did you feel as
you ran to your parent? Where did you feel that in your body? These
feelings are important.

Later, maybe you had a coach, a teacher, an older sibling, a
grandparent, or an aunt who delighted in you and you were able
to internalize their love. Or maybe later you had a loving spouse.
Again, you were able to receive their attunement and experience
the constancy of companionship, and this slowly rewired your brain
until the pathways changed. You moved toward a secure attachment. This is what psychologists call an earned secure attachment
because it was not received in the first few years of your life. Interestingly enough, we can have different attachment styles with
different caregivers.

What Does Attachment Look like for Adults?

As you read these lists of characteristics, which attachment style
resonates with you the most?

Insecure anxious/ambivalent (called preoccupied in adulthood):

- You fear abandonment.
- You sometimes struggle to find room for big feelings. It
  feels like you sometimes need to use lots of words and
  volume to feel heard or you feel like you need to keep your
  own needs silent.
- You control situations in order to keep yourself safe. This
  includes having a charm offensive and people pleasing. In
  fact, people pleasing is often a trauma response to feeling
  unsafe.

- You are always on the alert for any sign that you are going to be rejected or abandoned. You feel safer when you have one step out the door.

Insecure avoidant (called dismissive in adulthood):

- You struggle to name or even be aware of emotions.
- You stay in your head space when others want to talk about emotions. When someone shares their day, you want to fix, advise, or generally make them okay. Being in the presence of emotion often makes you feel uncomfortable.
- You feel unsafe being vulnerable.
- You self-protect by blaming, fixing, shutting down, appeasing, convincing, defending, snapping, retreating, distracting, and disassociating.
- You may have never learned that a relationship can be safe *and* go through conflict.

Insecure disorganized (adult with unresolved trauma):[6]

- Your behavior is unpredictable when connecting with others.
- Your inner life is chaotic.
- You need to disassociate often in order to feel safe.
- You sometimes struggle to trust others or even to know what trust means.
- You feel scared and insecure. It's a pendulum swing between trying to grasp for love and using avoidant behaviors.

Secure:

- Your body experiences secure attachment as a sense of ease. You feel safe and confident in most spaces.
- This may not be true 100 percent of the time, but you know how to get back to home base. You are able to move through difficult emotions on your own and with others,

moving from emotional dysregulation (or feeling amped up) back to regulation and a sense of safety.

- You can hold sorrow and joy at the same time.
- You feel loved even when you're not in the presence of your attachment person.
- You are empathetic and open to connection, able to attune to others.
- You are secure with others and able to focus energy on other parts of your life.
- You are vulnerable, able to take risks in relationships, and able to share your inner life with others.

Healing Attachment Wounds

The good news is that your attachment style is not set in concrete. The healing of an attachment wound is a journey. Our brains *can* transform, and our attachment wounds *can* heal. How? Through loving, supportive relationships and learning to live from the secure arms of Divine Love. These two are inextricably intertwined. Our attachment becomes more secure in community where our vulnerability is honored and our stories are safe.[7] We get in the jet stream of God's healing when we grow together.

Secure attachment is the goodness of God in the land of the living. It's Edenic. It's what we were created for. Emmanuel came to draw sons and daughters to His table on a cosmic mission to adopt us into His heart. Zephaniah 3:17 gives us a pathway of attachment with God:

"The LORD your God is with you."

This is the first condition to our ability to attach to God, and it's the basis of what this book is about. Until we know God is present, attentive, and turned toward us, we won't believe He's available for attachment. Practicing the truth of Emmanuel's nearness is primary.

Zephaniah also tells us God is "the Mighty Warrior who saves." In Ephesians 1:19–20, Paul reminds us that the Spirit who raised

Christ from the dead is the same Spirit living in you. Let's just pause there for a beat. Place one hand on your heart and one on your stomach and think about that. Love empowered lives within you, and He finds ecstatic joy in resurrecting impossible stories. You don't need to try to riddle all this out in your own limited power. The Holy Spirit is intimately acquainted with your story. Swing wide your arms and then invite Him to lead your journey with an ancient Pentecost prayer, "Come, Holy Spirit, come." And then daily, put your small hand in His.

"He will take great delight in you."

Receiving God's delight is not a trivial desire; it is paramount. In fact, our attachment with God is dependent on delight. We will not attach to someone we believe just tolerates our presence.[8] Friend, you are not a waste of His time. He is not dragging you through the world, annoyed with the dead weight. I love hearing God's obvious delight of Benjamin in Deuteronomy 33:12: "[He is] GOD's beloved; GOD's permanent residence. Encircled by GOD all day long, within whom GOD is at home" (MSG).

Zephaniah 3:17 ends with this phrase: "He will exult over you with loud singing" (ESV).

Until we have tuned our ears to hear the songs God sings over us with delight and until we learn to watch for His eyes sparkling when He looks our direction, we will find ourselves drawn to the eyes of passing strangers, wondering if we are desirable. Until we have a felt sense of attunement, comfort, care, and delight, we will keep riffling through the garbage looking for love where we found it last.

Living from God's Firm Embrace

Over time, as you engage in the attachment practices in the second half of the book, you will root and establish yourself in God's love, experience God holding you in your suffering, and discover both new and ancient ways to encounter the risen Christ through the Scriptures. Finally, God will begin to transform your warped images of His caregiving, which have been stuck in your relationship with your original caregiver. In God's firm embrace, your nervous system will come to experience "being quieted in God's love" (see Zeph 3:17 ESV). But, friends, all of this is dependent on our beginning to believe the promise of Emmanuel, that He is always present and available for us to run home to His arms.

But let's dial in a bit further and learn more about the attachment styles that have kept us stuck in cycles of anxiety and self-reliance. How have our early attachment experiences been both driving and stunting our relationship with God?

———

Access videos that explain how to create your upside-down triangle as well as a Lectio Divina practice on Zephaniah 3:17 at sum merjoygross.com/the-emmanuel-promise.

2

Insecure Anxious Attachment

What is insecure anxious attachment?

Psychologist Jock Gordon describes the insecure anxious attachment this way: "Deep down, an anxious-insecure adult's worst fear is that of abandonment and rejection. So, they try to control it by staying close to their partner, but this often comes across as clingy and needy. What's more, due to their needs being met inconsistently as a child, they might act over-emotional at times and exhibit poor self-control because they never feel as important and valuable as their partner."[1]

Some attributes of an insecure anxious attachment are:

- You struggle to feel "good enough."
- You strive to feel worthy of love.
- You tend to think of others as more important than yourself.
- You seek constant reassurance.
- You need attention and approval.
- You fear rejection or abandonment (for someone better, especially as that person gets to know the "true" you).
- You overthink and tend to take things personally, analyzing and being oversensitive.

- You exhibit fawning or people-pleasing behavior to prevent rejection.
- You are caring and kind, often at the cost of your own well-being.[2]

Somewhere along the way, I picked up the belief that I had to work for love by managing my presence in a room, hoping I exhibited a winning personality and trying to anticipate others' needs. I believed I had to squeeze my shoulders tight, to make myself small, to not cause "a fuss." This same belief was carried over into my relationship with God. I thought I had to make myself presentable, worthy of God's response. Many of us get stuck in our relationship with God, practicing our smile in the mirror, repeating our memory verses for gold stars. God wants us to look happy, right?

We think we need to make ourselves Sunday-morning presentable as we cover up the needs of a heart that is exceedingly weary. We are practicing perfect while God desires us to practice the art of authentically crying out.

As insecure anxious attachment types, we tend to keep our cries inside until one is weighed on a scale of merit and believed worthy of God's attention. Once upon a time, we did not weigh our needs or cover them up.

If only we had armor against need itself, we think. We glance at others who look like they have it "all together" and then back at ourselves, wishing we were steadier.

But the self-reliant individual who doesn't need love and connection is a myth. Often, the self-reliant individual has lost hope that love and connection are on offer. We'll talk about that more in the next chapter.

Humans were wired to be "needy." It was a part of our creation. If we were never hungry, we would not search for bread. If we did not need love, we would not move toward each other.

Neediness is a God-given invitation to connection and communion.[3] God wanted to create a braided world of mutual care.

He also wanted us to need Him and to desire attachment. But attachment cannot be formed without awareness of need.

Friend, in the middle of your longing, this is what I want you to understand: Your need is not a negative. Your need is an invitation to cry out and search your environment for love. For the insecure anxious attached, your need may make you feel broken and grasping. You wonder if you will ever experience *enough*. Instead, what if I told you that your need is a runway to becoming a healed, whole person with a secure attachment?

A Different Invitation

It was January in upstate New York, and outside the windows were whiteout conditions. Great-grandpa Ralph pulled on large boots, leather gloves, and a thick, knitted wool hat. His animals still needed to be fed and watered, despite the weather. He must have gotten disoriented as the blizzard whipped and pulled at his clothes, snow adhering to every inch of uncovered skin, searing. The wind took his breath away, along with any internal compass, and somehow it pushed him west until he stepped onto the rotted beams covering the old well. He slid down the sides and found himself knee-deep in water. Not good. People died in old wells. In July.

He was quickly swallowed by the dark and as he tried to hoist himself up the side of the embedded stones, his boots kept sliding down each toehold. "Don't panic. You can't panic," he kept repeating to himself. I don't know if he prayed, but I can't imagine that he didn't cry out. Over time, an unexpected thought occurred to him: *What if I allow my glove to freeze to the side of the well? If the wet glove freezes hard, I can use it as a lever to hoist myself up.* It must have taken hours, hours of waiting and trying to keep himself warm, rubbing his hands together to create warmth. Eventually, the frozen glove gave him the handhold he needed, and after pulling himself up, he fought his way back to the farmhouse, where Great-grandma Pearl nervously awaited his return.

Just like my great-grandpa in the storm, we can become confused by need, dysregulated, and unable to see ourselves clearly. When our cavernous need is triggered, we feel the disorientation of a whiteout, the pain of an icy blizzard, the fear of not being able to get ourselves home. We fear our bottomless need the way Great-grandpa feared freezing inside the old well.

What if we were invited not to escape the need but to become acquainted with it? What if we were invited to become curious and compassionate with the way this sometimes overwhelming need to feel safe, seen, soothed, and secure was created?

God-Given Longing

The following is a gentle invitation to become acquainted with what this primal longing feels like. We often pass over this step, becoming immediately reactive and reaching. We want to stuff the ache with accessible comfort. We can interrupt our lurching toward love, belonging, and worth when we learn to pay attention to and turn toward it with curiosity and compassion.

> When do you lurch toward love, belonging, and worth? Pay attention to this.
>
> When do you get angry or jealous when someone else is "stealing" the love, belonging, or worth you crave?
>
> What happens right before?
>
> What feelings are connected to this overwhelming need? How do they feel in your body?
>
> When you feel the ache, your need for love, belonging, and worth, what longings make you reactive instead of responsive?
>
> When you desire to feel seen, to feel delighted in, to feel the warmth of care, what does it feel like? Describe it in an image. Where do you feel it in your body? Is there a

heaviness on your chest? Does fear of loneliness feel like a punch in the gut? When shame and need are woven together, we often feel it in our stomach. Does it feel like a hollowness? An emptiness? A weight?

When this need rises with ferocity as during an extended season of loneliness or relational conflict, I feel this ache in my stomach, as if I've been punched in the gut. Then, when I'm afraid of abandonment, I'll wake up from sleep with a wave of nausea and a need to move.

Before you participate in shame's campaign, turning away from your own needs, remember: your longings are good, God-given even. All of your needs would have been met in the garden of Eden, a dance of constant care between you, God, and the beautiful creations—human or otherwise—He created as your companions. Need draws us toward each other. We were meant to be engaged in a dance of giving and receiving.

Our need was given to braid us into the loving care of the Trinity.

Your Needs Were Never a Liability

Remember, you were created for secure attachment. In those first three years after you emerged from the womb, you were created to cry out liberally, allowing your need to be known. Crying out was your job. Without a cry, there can be no response. Without a cry, no one knows you are hungry.

Hopefully, when you cried out in the first few years of your life, you soon saw your mother's face peering in: "I'm here, little one. Don't worry. I've got you." She watched you for a moment, reading your signals, before finally picking you up. She'd quiet your wail, bouncing you a little bit, shushing in your ear. A secure attachment is built slowly, with one met need after another until trust is developed. You needed milk so she fed you, her arm under your head, her eyes gazing into yours.

Perhaps you had an experience that looked like this; perhaps you didn't. The quality of your attachment with your first caregiver was created in those first few years of crying out and experiencing a timely response.

Right now, what I want you to hear is this: your attachment was never your responsibility.[4] The quality of your bond was the sole responsibility of your caregiver, and that bond set you up for how smooth the road to building trust was, not just in that relationship, but in all your relationships.

The world looked plenteous or scarce based on the trust built between you and your caregiver. Your responsibility was never to weigh the level of your need and decide if it was worthy of care. Your responsibility was only to cry out. We'll come back to that later.

Each of your needs was a gift along the pathway to a secure attachment. Here's a list of the core longings and needs you were given by God for His vision of a braided life together:

- a safe and secure environment
- constant reinforcement of personal worth
- repeated messages that you are valued, unique, and special
- unconditional love and acceptance
- basic care and nurturing
- encouragement to grow and develop personal gifts and talents
- a pathway to fellowship with God
- a sense of belonging
- a feeling of usefulness and being needed[5]

How We Cope

When core longings and needs were not met in our family of origin, our past experiences created our future expectations. Our bodies have long memories of living in the wasteland of need. They become so sure our needs won't be met that we build a host of coping mechanisms in order to provide for ourselves.

Here's an illustration from people who experienced food poverty during the Great Depression. Although they are now able to go to the grocery store and purchase what they need, when they have the first pangs of hunger, their body immediately remembers starvation, and instead of eating judiciously, they binge, making darn sure they won't feel that sense of hunger again. That hunger doesn't just speak of need now; it reminds them of lack then. It has less to do with food and more to do with a memory of struggle.[6]

For those of us afraid love will be measured out in teaspoons so we never feel full, as soon as we feel lonely as an adult, we may manipulate ways to stay close to our loved one, demanding attention. We will do anything to reduce the space between ourselves and the felt reality of not enough.

So, here are a few questions to better acquaint you with the depth of your need:

When you feel the ache of longing and the fear that it won't be filled, what are you tempted to do to fill that need?

Do you guard the pit (the chasm of need), cover the pit, or fill the pit?

Do you guard the pit with a gate, making sure you don't get close to the need?

Maybe you guard the ache with a well-devised ego. You fashion a barrier out of today's trendy styles or a list of successes or the ability to read others to see how your perfectly designed persona is coming across. Or you protect yourself with a library of information. Perhaps you self-protect with a well-honed capacity to care for others and make them feel loved.

Or maybe you protect yourself from overwhelming need by caring for yourself through manipulation, control, people pleasing, perfection, or performance.

Maybe you have such quick coping mechanisms you can pretend the ache doesn't exist. You try to *cover* the need with escapism: binge-watching TV or downing a glass of wine, scrolling Instagram for a false sense of community, or just lying down to sleep and turning off the world.

The ache is so uncomfortable that you work to get good at mastering your felt need, pretending it doesn't exist.

But Emmanuel Draws Closer

In order to develop a new healthy attachment, we need a safe place for our ache to come to the surface.

The Samaritan woman came to the well with the type of ache for love that was cavernous. If she dropped a pebble in the well, it would take a long time to hit bottom. Remember, her need was given to braid her to others. Her need was given to braid her into the love of the Trinity.

Jesus was waiting for her at the well with a divine appointment and an invitation to allow her need to find His offering. Can you imagine how she must have felt in the presence of His full attention? It must have been a healing of its own.

Jesus sent His disciples away to hunt for bread, creating a safe place for her story and her ache to come to the surface. The two of them were at the well, a strange congregation—one Jew, one Samaritan. One man, a rabbi, and a woman who was living outside the conventions of society. One holding a waterskin but with cavernous need. One without a bucket but with a never-ending capacity to hold her need.

"Everyone who drinks this water will be thirsty again," Jesus pointed out, "but whoever drinks the water I give them will never thirst. Indeed, the water I give them will become in them a spring of water welling up to eternal life."

Then, after whetting her appetite, He invited her need to the surface: "Go, call your husband and come back."

"I have no husband," she told Him.

Jesus replied, "You are right when you say you have no husband. The fact is, you have had five husbands, and the man you now have is not your husband. What you have just said is quite true."[7]

Jesus wants us to bring our need into His presence with clarity, not to guard, attempt to fill, or escape it. We don't have to shrink or manage our need to make it acceptable. The God of the universe has unlimited capacity to hold our need with tenderness.

Jesus saw the Samaritan woman's yearning for love and didn't keep His distance. He wasn't scared. He wasn't surprised. He drew closer.

Her need for love had left her life looking like a field hit by enemy fire. One marriage after another had blown up in her face, yet her need drove her to seek the next one. Sometimes people with insecure anxious attachment believe someone else's desire for them is the answer that will fill the ache within.

But Jesus sees your need and does not keep His distance.

He is not scared of your need.

He's not surprised by your need.

He created your need.

Attachment is developed because a need is expressed and filled. Your cry becomes the invitation. His response builds trust.

When you let your need cry out, He draws closer.

Dear One, let your need become a beacon for God. A runway.

Maybe you don't collect marriages like the Samaritan woman; maybe you collect Pinterest-worthy houses or locations and you move from new neighborhood to new neighborhood, hopeful of the promise of connection. Or churches. Or bars. Maybe you collect friends whose neediness causes you to feel wanted.

Or maybe you collect degrees with the hope that someone will stand up and take notice. Or promotions. Or accolades. Or likes on Instagram.

I love that Jesus met the Samaritan woman at the well and did not back away from her need or gloss over the aching truth of it.

He met her in the middle of her shame. He invited the pain of her story into His presence.

Need can be confusing. A longing for love can often feel like physical hunger or thirst, an empty stomach. Our body is a map of need, but sometimes the GPS is unclear. We might reach for the refrigerator when what we're really hungry for is connection. Emotions are embodied, but that doesn't mean they are straightforward.

Let's explore the Samaritan woman's story a little further. Could it be that the Samaritan woman, although a real flesh-and-blood person, was also the fulfillment of an archetype of Israel meeting her Beloved in the flesh? This may seem like a detour, but I promise we're headed toward a feast. A metaphor is woven throughout the Old Testament of God's desire for Israel and her unfaithfulness as she looked everywhere but toward God for connection. Like an expert weaver of stories, God invites the Samaritan woman to represent Israel and, indeed, all of our insecure anxious hearts. Jesus was introducing the wandering Israel to the only One who could truly meet her needs unconditionally.

Here's an example from Jeremiah: "My people have exchanged their glorious God for worthless idols. . . . They have forsaken me, the spring of living water, and have dug their own cisterns, broken cisterns that cannot hold water" (2:11, 13).

The story of the prophet Hosea and his wife, Gomer, a prostitute he was instructed to marry as an illustration of God's love to an unfaithful Israel, has the same bass line and melody. Gomer had a commitment, compassion, and provision problem, so she kept going back to old lovers to get her needs met.

Whether we've lived with food poverty or love poverty, experiencing lack may send us into panic mode, grasping and gorging, even when we have a vow of provision from God.

Gomer was promised provision by her husband, but her body didn't yet trust that she was safe. She hadn't built new neural pathways of cry and response. Unfortunately, her brain had decades to establish the scaffolding of another story.

Fear can lead us to self-destruct. It can lead us to destroy the beautiful because we imagine a story of pain. It can also lead us to hurt those closest to us. Have you heard the line, "Hurt people hurt people"? It's true. In many cases, the fear-induced actions of trauma-holders can leave behind a minefield of pain.

Fear of lack can also lead us to destroy new possibilities resident in our relationships. We get good at running down the same path to self-provision as if scarcity is chasing us. It's familiar. The neural pathways are established. The path pulls us to what is known and feels safe.

Forming New Attachments

Let's up the ante. What if the neural pathway of lack has been established for generations? Our attachment style can get written into our DNA. For example, even the children of those who grew up during the Great Depression can live in a house of scarcity. Or think about Jacob's children who were stuck as slaves in Egypt for four hundred years. When they were hungry, they were pulled back to what felt known and safe. We do the same. We get pulled back into relationships that repeat. We might marry a new person, but it's often the same story.

We are tempted to sneer at the children of Israel wandering in the desert, but if we remember that slavery and scarcity paved the neural pathways of unmet needs, we may become more compassionate. After four hundred years of living in Egypt, the children of Israel had expectations of absence. What did God do? He led them out into the desert. In Hosea 2:14, God says, "I will allure her, and bring her into the wilderness, and speak tenderly to her" (ESV).

In the darkness they *had* to turn toward God with their cries, asking again and again, Are you there for me? Do you see me? Will you be there for me in the future?

When new attachments need to be formed, the desert is oddly our friend. It's where emptiness becomes fullness. It's where we learn to "leave and cleave."

At Home with the Trinity

We often don't understand the level of our attachment wounds until fissures begin to show. C. S. Lewis said, "We can ignore pleasure, but pain insists upon being attended to. God whispers to us in our pleasures, speaks in our conscience, but shouts in our pains: it is his megaphone to rouse a deaf world."[8]

Sometimes it takes the opening of a wound in order to create the right environment for healing. It can be excruciating bringing pain out into the open. My own pain came from a midlife fear of abandonment. As I moved through this journey of healing from an insecure attachment, I spent mornings in front of the fireplace, my own chosen place of silence. I would say goodbye to the children for the morning, turn on the gas fireplace, make a hot cup of tea, and open a journal and Bible. I'd read. I'd scratch down a few lines. Mostly, I would wait, bringing the lanced wound out before God. The solitude of those hours became my desert as I forced myself to sit still. Open. Waiting.

In the middle of some of my worst fears of abandonment, I was given this prayer image: I was the match girl, emaciated, hair matted, wearing wet, ragged clothes. As I climbed a long flight of stone stairs, shivering, suddenly a large wooden door flew open. Abba God filled the doorway. "Welcome home," He said as He laughed, His arms out, gently ushering me inside.

As I peeked around the corner, I saw a round, stone room with a series of couches facing a huge stone fireplace. A fire snapped and fizzled and roared, warming the room. I held my hands out to the fire.

Motioning for me to sit on a chaise lounge facing the fire, Abba put both hands on its back and I, wrecked, dirty, and exhausted, sat down, sinking into the cushions and pulling my legs up toward the warmth of the fire. He then wrapped me in a long, fur blanket, tucking me in and bringing me a mug of hot tea to warm my hands. Occasionally, He placed a hand on my shoulder as we chatted while

He fussed over a tea table. Emmanuel sat cross-legged in front of the fire with me. Kindness exuded from Him. I leaned back and rested, smelling the black tea in my mug. The Holy Spirit sat on a long, round couch that extended around the room like a hug. He was quiet, too, but no less present.

I took deep breaths, feeling the warmth of the mug through my fingers, and rested in the care of the Trinity.

I was at home. The Trinity had moved into the pit, put up curtains, and started a fire, and no matter how much I wandered outside the security of that room, there was always an open invitation to come back home. The cavern had become a sanctuary.

Friend, you may find yourself outside love, standing at the edge of a gaping cavern, or still trying to guard, fill, or escape the pit. Yet, as Eugene Peterson paraphrased in John 1:14, God has "moved into the neighborhood" (MSG). Your need is not too much. Your need is just the right environment for attachment. You are invited to cry out and watch Him respond.

Or maybe all of this talk of emotions and pits and cavernous need feels awkward. That's, as we say in spiritual direction, just good information. Do you find yourself annoyed with the invitation to cry out? You've been taught that you need to be strong and stalwart. You've been taught that having needs makes you vulnerable to attack. Let's sit with that. Maybe you'll find helpful information in the next chapter.

Push play on a video at summerjoygross.com/the-emmanuel-promise and listen while I invite you to walk into the story of Jesus with the Samaritan woman. Then join me as I lead you in a Lectio Divina of Jeremiah 2:11 and 13.

3

Insecure Avoidant Attachment

What does it mean to have an insecure avoidant attachment? Therapists speculate that the insecure avoidant individual is an insecure anxious individual who has entirely lost hope. They came to believe that no one was coming.

If this is your attachment style, it is highly likely your caregiver often questioned your needs. Maybe you came into the kitchen hungry and your caregiver said something like, "You're not hungry. You just ate." Or perhaps you were fed and bathed, but no one was paying attention to your inner life, tuning in, and comforting you when you needed the warmth of arms around you.

The messages you heard may have sounded like this:

- Nightmares? "Cry it out."
- Pain? "Grit it out."
- Feeling boisterous and playful? "Children should be seen and not heard."
- Angry, frustrated, or just reaching for connection? "Don't whine."

The list could go on and on. The point is that when you ran to the arms of your caregiver, expecting a soft place to land, you encountered an emotional wall.

Every child needs someone "tuned in," someone to wait patiently and to tenderly hold them as the storm of feelings shifts and sorts and makes its way through. They need someone to lean in, to listen, to stay in the storm with them until it starts to subside.

To understand, not fix.

To settle, not dismiss.

To soothe, not tranquilize.

If you are insecure avoidant attached, maybe you had a moment when you decided to show your brave little heart and the need you carried, but at that moment, it was clear your need was treated as a problem to be solved, not an invitation to connection. Because of this, you began to believe, "My full self is not desired in the room. I have to tone it down. I can only show what's acceptable." And so you did. You numbed. You quieted your tender inner life in exchange for a feeling of internal safety. You exchanged understanding for self-preservation.

Or perhaps your caregiver's love came with requirements. You didn't have time to be a child because you were caring for them. Or you weren't able to experience love because, in order to experience attachment, there were rules upon rules upon rules, some spoken, most inferred. If you stepped out of line, they turned away. Shame was a weapon until you modified your behavior. You weren't taught to behave, but you were punished for not following unspoken conventions. You never felt like it was acceptable to grow, to be imperfect, to learn, to make mistakes. Love and belonging were conditional on your behavior.

Because of this, you missed being celebrated just for being. You didn't know what it felt like to be delighted in, to be enjoyed. And so you turned inside, became self-reliant, and cultivated shields of strength. You amassed an arsenal to protect yourself, and while you felt safe inside your fortress, unfortunately, you were also alone inside those walls. Because the softness needed for love felt unsafe, you rarely admitted your loneliness to yourself. The armor of self-protection was just too necessary.

Here are some characteristics of the insecure avoidant attached:

- You are convinced that you are alone and have to project strength.
- You minimize your emotions. Numbing is safety. Also, you dismiss others' emotions.
- You shut yourself off from need and intimacy. You believe the less need you have, the less you will find yourself alone.
- You push people away when they get too close and are afraid of "being found out."
- You experience vulnerability as a weakness, not a strength.
- You struggle to trust. You feel most comfortable being self-reliant, not depending on others.
- You easily swing toward judgment instead of being self-reflective and humble.
- You wear masks as coping mechanisms for protection.
- You have a strong inner critic that is usually the internalized voice of your caregiver.
- You build masks and false ego selves, feeling safer having someone encounter your "perfect," well-designed self.[1]

Remember the Strange Situation experiment from chapter 1? Sometimes the mother would walk out the door and the child would remain inside, comfortably playing, barely looking up. She'd come back in, and the child might glance her direction or might not. The child didn't seem to notice. There was no sense of need. When the mom walked back into the room, she wouldn't call out to the child or invite the child to cuddle or connect. The child was happy. Why interrupt? This is the story of the insecure avoidant child. They are self-reliant and believe alone is safer than connected.

Never forget that it is the caregiver who is the one responsible for the attachment. Children react; they do not create attachments. If you were shamed for the lack of bond with your caregiver, you can lay that down now. It was not your fault.

Perhaps growing up, your caregiver ran your house like an efficient clock, without time for emotions, their own or anyone else's. You stopped reaching out. You stopped listening for the sound of their shoes in the next room. You became enclosed, focused on meeting your own needs. This may have happened early on. Or this may have happened later in life.

Sometimes, because of death, mental illness, depression, divorce, or sickness, the one you counted on early in life was suddenly no longer available. The familiar pattern of cry and response was shut down. Comfort was withheld. The smile of delight that was characteristic of your life together became Still Face. You may have still occupied the same places at the table, but suddenly you were living in unfamiliar territory.

Perhaps you learned to weigh your need on a scale created by a capricious caregiver. If you played your cards just right, at the right time of day or with the right kind of need, the caregiver would turn toward you.

However it came to be, through thousands of interactions with your caregiver, you discerned comfort and care were not available. The home base of your caregiver's love was not secure. You were not safe.

Stories of Insecure Avoidant Attachment

I asked members of my Presence Project community who have an insecure avoidant attachment to share their stories. Here are just a few:

Heather

Heather was a missionary kid. The oldest of four kids in her home, she was homeschooled by a mom who was emotionally unavailable. Her dad, often angry, was the only one who was allowed to have emotions in their home.

Heather often heard, "Stop crying or I'll give you something to cry about."

She quickly learned to numb her emotions and kept herself safe by being hyper-responsible. This became the norm in her relationship with God as well. Learning all the verses. Keeping her needs at a minimum.

Sharon

Sharon's home was organized and quiet, emphasis on quiet. It was the picture of Southern charm. After Sharon snuck out of the house one night with a friend, her mother didn't speak to her for six months. Sharon became self-reliant, but her mother's voice became the sound of her own inner critic, always present, always grating. Discordant but familiar.

Not until Sharon began attending a women's Bible study small group did she notice the words the other women used to describe God: *loving, merciful, caring.* She was shocked. Did they really believe that or was it an act? When she did something wrong, she had to put herself into a pretzel, giving herself various punishments until she could wear a "facade of trustworthiness" with God, beginning to earn His approval. She saw Him as easily angry and capricious. Just like her mom.

Erin

Erin shared this insight on her attachment style: "My attachment style led to hyper-independence, which caused a dual way of thinking about God: God is going to eventually abandon me (if He hasn't already) so I better just take on everything on my own (leading to a need to control and anticipate everything in order to feel safe) AND my issues and prayers were too burdensome for Him (there are always people in greater pain, greater need, and greater turmoil than me) so I repress and stuff it all away, leading to a disconnection from self (because the pain of being on my own is just too unbearable) and God (because of the walls I built around myself that were meant for protection but became my own prison)."

Just as an aside, we can form different bonds with different caregivers—an insecure anxious attachment with a mother or an insecure avoidant with a father. Remember, an attachment just measures *the quality* of your bond. Whether this is the case or not, we come out of early childhood with a primary attachment style that will be a pattern for later engagement.

Masks of the Insecure Avoidant

Here are a few of the masks an insecure avoidant person puts on to keep themself safe. These are stories I've collected from dear people from the Presence Project. Each story highlights a mask someone with insecure avoidant attachment may choose to wear.

Staying Busy: Julie

This is what Julie shared about being insecure avoidant: "You find ways to stay busy so you can avoid putting in the work to sit and be still and position yourself with Christ, which creates distance and more of a reason to avoid Him. It's a tough cycle to break sometimes. But taking that first step of leaning in to Christ can break the cycle, and then you find His presence glorious, refreshing, and rewarding. But facing the thing you work hard to avoid isn't easy. It usually stirs up a lot of emotion for me."

Numbing Needs and Being Silenced: Sharon, Christine, and Barbara

Sharon told me: "It seems like I often haven't even had the thought to look to Him for help. Like it doesn't even enter my consciousness as a possibility to ask."

Christine numbed for a different reason: "As the oldest child, I often felt growing up that my 'hard' emotions were too much for my parents. Instead of helping me learn to regulate myself, I was often helping my parents regulate themselves."

Barbara shared this: "For so long I thought God was distant, harsh, and uninterested in the details of my life. I was so wrong. He has been slowly unfolding memories with me and showing me where He was in those tough places and how He provided in ways I had not even realized."

Not Getting Close and Staying in Head Knowledge: Shelby

This is what Shelby shared: "My unknown insecure [avoidant] attachment kept me from being emotionally and spiritually intimate with the Lord and with others. It was only when the Lord brought this and my avoidant attachment style to light that I realized I never really knew intimacy with the Lord. I wasn't able to recognize my own heart and emotions so, therefore, I wasn't able to share them with the Lord. Although He knew, it changed everything when I was able to recognize, name, and lay down my emotions at His feet. It has changed everything to be able to invite the Spirit into areas of my heart that I would rather push away or previously would have ignored. It has taken the walls around my heart being broken down to get to know myself. Through learning about myself, I am opening myself to our Creator. I am learning how He has uniquely created my brain in contrast to how the world has corrupted it. I feel as though I have begun to live a new life since beginning the journey of healing my avoidant attachment. It has only drawn me closer to the Lord and made me fall more in love with Him. It was a depth I never knew I was missing."

I love that comment from Shelby. So many people never know that intimacy is missing from their relationship. They've lost hope of a loving Father, possibly because of their insecure avoidant attachment, possibly because of how they were introduced to God. If our churches only stay in a left-brained, intellectual vein, we don't have someone to position us to experience an encounter with the love of God. We may have been promised a relationship but quickly dialed down our expectations.

What We Learn about Vulnerability from Thomas Merton

Another way an avoidant person keeps themself safe is by refusing to be vulnerable. This can look like overconfidence, pride, or the inner discipline of a rule follower. They use control to counter insecurity. In their family of origin, it may have looked something like this, "If I learn all the rules and do everything right, I'll stay safe."

This same desire for inner perfection can keep them from the humility needed for vulnerable connection and love-based obedience to God. This may look like amassing wealth or hyperfocusing on their career—anything that might create a facade of success, a tower of Babel to prove their strength, whether in ministry or in other vocations. To this, theologian Thomas Merton says, "The man who is not afraid to admit everything that he sees to be wrong with himself, and yet recognizes that he may be the object of God's love, can begin to be sincere. His sincerity is based on confidence, not in his own illusions about himself, but in the endless, unfailing mercy of God."[2]

Thomas Merton, a prolific spiritual writer, called these and other ways of protecting himself the false ego self. Remember the little one who didn't acknowledge the mother as she came back into the room during the Strange Situation experiment? Way before the experiment took place, that precious soul had to work hard to create their own sense of internal safety. If they didn't look their mother's way, they wouldn't see Still Face looking back. The child stiff-armed connection in exchange for stoicism, though it may have been only for show, to shrink their needs to keep the peace. I think Thomas Merton, one of the greatest spiritual life writers of the twentieth century, would understand this child's need for self-protection. It's something Thomas had to learn early as well.

Thomas Merton's mother wrote him a short, handwritten letter from her hospital bed, informing him that she was dying and that he wouldn't see her again. He took the letter under his favorite tree to read. In his autobiography, *The Seven Storey Mountain*, Merton describes his mother as "demanding intellectual perfection, worried, precise, quick, and critical of me, her son." He was only six when she passed away.

Until he entered the monastery at twenty-seven, Merton lived in a hodgepodge of houses and boarding schools, sometimes with his father, often without. His father, a painter of the lost generation, was always eager for the next exhibition in New York or London, and he would dismantle his son's life without a thought of how it might affect him. As soon as Thomas became comfortable in a new place, he would be whisked away to an unfamiliar destination. Upon seeing his son in grief during one of these upheavals, Merton's father dismissed his emotions, essentially saying, "Dry your tears. Why wouldn't a boy want to move to France?" His father died when Merton was only sixteen.

In *The Seven Storey Mountain*, Merton includes a vignette about a lovely farming couple in Murat, France. He was sent to the Privats' home because he had been struggling with an illness for months at a boarding school that had all the warmth and nurture of a prison. The Privats fed him "milk and butter" and nursed him back to health. During this time, his dad was away, painting in Paris. "Those were weeks that I shall never forget," Merton wrote. "The more I think of them, the more I realize I must certainly owe the Privats for more than butter and milk and good nourishing food for my body. They treated me as their own child." Then he added, "As a child, and since then too, I have always tended to resist any kind of a possessive affection on the part of any other human being—there has always been this profound instinct to keep clear, to keep free." The Privats' love "did not burn you, it did not hold you, it did not try to imprison you in demonstrations, or trap your feet in the snares of its interest."[3] He even wondered if he owed his eventual conversion to Christ to the kindness of their prayers.

What's most clear about Thomas Merton's attachment was that, until he landed in the monastery, he had lost hope in finding a secure base. His years at Clare College–Cambridge, after his father's death, were filled with a particular lostness that included drinking, getting bailed out of prison by his guardian for hotel room debts, and having a child he never acknowledged with a woman he never married.

Merton took a vow of stability at the age of twenty-seven when he entered into the Abbey of Gethsemani in Kentucky. Although it's impossible to be sure whether he was avoidantly attached, his spiritual writings are sprinkled with the wrestling of someone who understands this attachment style. He writes brilliantly of the manufacturing of the false ego self as a way of protection. He recognizes that false ego self must be dismantled because only the vulnerable kernel of the true self can experience the tenderness of being God's beloved.

As he came into a daily relationship with one place and one community, Merton slowly put down roots. He had an abbot who encouraged his writing, a spiritual director who held his story with wisdom and attunement, weekly confession, a practice of naming inner realities in a safe place, and a daily rhythm of chanting the Psalms. Slowly, he began to experience inner stability.

The practice of the presence of God was woven throughout his days in highly practical ways. Merton was called to prayer seven times a day so, together, he and the other monks could pray the Psalms and other prayers in the Liturgy of the Hours. Like all Trappists, the bell would ring, the men would gather in the chapel, rain or shine, night or day. Alongside them, Merton would chant, his nervous system finding peace as he took a daily journey through the Psalms. Together, the brothers witnessed David, the psalmist who wrote as one securely attached with God, regulate his emotions through uncensored lament and praise. Even witnessing another person regulating their emotion and watching their attachment to God can become an example we mirror. Maybe through chanting the Psalms, as well as through writing about his internal world, Merton came to understand that his emotions are always welcomed in the presence of God, and the ultimate freedom, his true self under all the layers of self-protection, is beloved.

What can we learn from Merton's story? Although he had to manufacture levels of self-protection as a child, becoming honest about his story through writing, practicing emotional awareness through the Psalms, and rooting in a community, he began to find a home base in the heart of God. Slowly, he removed his protective barrier and experienced a sense of belonging.

The beauty of how God designed our brains is that no matter how deep the patterns of self-protection and hiding go, there is always hope. Our insecure attachment can be transformed. Our minds are able to be renewed.[4] We don't need to join a monastery to experience the healing of God, but we can learn from Merton's story.

Insecure Avoidant Attachment in the Bible

Although self-reliance may reflect the coping mechanisms of an insecure avoidant person desperately trying to establish inner safety, when we become a child of God, this same tendency echoes an ancient lie: God withholds. I must provide for myself. It may also cause us to wonder if He has our best interests at heart. Perhaps Eve was the very first insecure avoidant, not yet trusting she was secure in the arms of God. Recognizing this internal lie of the need for self-provision can open the way to attachment with God.

Before communion was broken between God and humanity, before the fruit was taken, Adam and Eve lived and breathed inside a garden that represented the promise of God's presence. It was a space designed for companionship, every created thing a part of a feast of communion between God and Adam and Eve. Every morning, they were refreshed in each other's presence. And can't you imagine that every evening, as they were "walking in the garden in the cool of the day," they recounted the joys of the day, pointing out what was blooming, what was ripe (Gen. 3:8). They obeyed the Sabbath invitation to "taste and see that the Lord is good" (Ps. 34:8).

They walked among His planted provisions. They were given jobs of naming and expanding. They breathed with His breath. They had each other. They had been given everything they could possibly need and then some.

Unfortunately, Eve stopped when she heard the serpent's hiss. "Why would God keep this slice of goodness from you?" he suggested. "He knows, if you eat this fruit, you will be like Him" (see Gen. 3). And for the first time, perhaps, they wondered if God was truly good. Was He withholding?

And this is what I can't get over. How long had it actually been since they had heard the warm tone of God's voice? Five minutes? Ten? How long does it take before *we* start believing the lies of scarcity from our attachment: I am alone. I have to provide for myself. When we lose the perspective of God's nearness, we begin to believe we have to provide for ourselves.

Their questions were revealed and, like children, they hid in the bushes, covering their bodies with leaves. But God's compassion literally never stopped. He took animal hide and needle and thread and fashioned clothes for the ones who had questioned His goodness, despite the feast of His abundance. I want you to hear this next point: when they lost the beauty of their garden, God's love never diminished.

The core questions in the middle of this story, Is God good? and Will God provide for me? were echoed in the wilderness between Egypt and Canaan, mile after desert mile. The presence of God was near, setting a table before them, but every day as they awoke, they lost the thread of God's goodness. Their brains had been formed by slavery and scarcity. They couldn't imagine the One who walked beside them was the One who was providing for them at every level. They often wondered if God really did have the ability to provide. As they lost hope in God's presence and provision and forged a golden calf, they fashioned a life they could control.

Self-provision and control. Maybe you too feel echoes of this story threaded throughout your own?

Moving toward Secure Attachment with Emmanuel

Where do we go from here? We can't all be monastics like Merton, nor can we jump into such a rigorous lifestyle. How do we start small? Here are three simple steps we can take to begin practicing the promise of Emmanuel right where we are.

1. **Begin by praying the simple prayer, "You are here."** Allow yourself to rest in the intellectual truth that God, the Emmanuel, is present, whether you *sense* His presence or not. He has promised to be present. We can stand firm on this truth.

2. **Know that God has been practicing your presence all along.** Let that sink in. Since you made your quiet entry into the world, safe in the haven of your mother's womb, God was practicing your presence. In Psalm 139, David makes this clear: "My frame was not hidden from you when I was made in the secret place, when I was woven together in the depths of the earth. Your eyes saw my unformed body; all the days ordained for me were written in your book before one of them came to be" (vv. 15–16).

   There was never one second when God was Still-Faced in your life. His face has always been shining toward you, even when you were a tiny mass of cells. He was there to receive you in the delivery room, throwing a party and showing you off. Always remember: when you turn toward Him, He is already turned toward you. He is always practicing *your* presence.

3. **Notice the emotions displayed through Scripture, especially in the Psalms and Gospels.** Then, begin to acknowledge the emotions you yourself are holding. Note what emotions David and the other psalmists are bringing before God. Consider using a journaling Bible and writing notes in the corner. When you read the Gospels, notice how Jesus experienced the whole range of human emotions: angry enough

to turn over tables, moved with compassion toward the crowd of five thousand, jumping up and down in joy when the disciples came back from their mission, fearful and questioning in the garden of Gethsemane, distraught enough to weep with Mary as He dove into the grief of a mother.

God has unlimited capacity to be with you in grief or depression, anger or fear. None of it is too much for Him. We have downgraded God's capacity because of the human capacity of our human caregivers. Yet God's strength to hold our heaviness and His ability to comfort are infinite. We don't need to weigh our needs on a human scale. What if I told you that God loves you as you are and enjoys your company, even though you're imperfect? Remember, the father of the prodigal son ran toward his boy as he hobbled toward home smelling of pigs. The father just wanted his boy HOME. The truth is that God wants to be a part of your transformation every step of the way, to comfort you and clean you up. He sees your masks and understands why you wear them, but He'd rather be with the real, unvarnished you. Not a watered-down version. Not a buttoned-up and scrubbed-clean version. Not a drawn-on, smiley-face rule follower. Just you. The masks you have worked so hard to fashion have become layers of walls between you and Him, one more way you keep Him at a distance. Allow Him full access into the middle of your imperfect story.

4

Insecure Disorganized Attachment

Sometimes our attachment styles are the result of significant trauma, and oh, Dear One, if that's you, I want you to know I'm so sorry for the story that has shaped you.

Often this attachment style is a sign that some type of abuse has occurred, either violence toward you by your caregiver or perhaps you witnessed abuse toward someone else by your caregiver. In any event, trust has been completely broken down. Your personality was shaped by fear. As I talked to folks who had this attachment style, I learned that the broken trust was usually the result of a caregiver who had some type of mental illness.

This is a short chapter, not because this attachment style is any less important but because it shows up in conflicting ways that are specific to each story. Children in Mary Ainsworth's Strange Situation experiment who have disorganized attachment often cried when their mother left the room.[1] Then, when she returned, they either avoided her or ran to her and froze. Sometimes they displayed truly odd behavior, like huddling in a corner as if they were being punished already, because of past experiences of abuse.[2] They knew their mother was the provider of food and they needed to stay close to be fed, but they also intuited that they needed to keep a safe distance. They had trauma responses, which dipped into both insecure anxious and insecure avoidant coping behaviors, and they may pendulum swing between them based on the mother's mood or their own emotions. When you read the other chapters, you may not have been able to put your finger on your own attachment style because of this lack of clarity. However, as you can imagine, if you have an insecure disorganized attachment, you may relate to the following characteristics:

- You internally battle between neediness and distance, often giving others mixed messages.
- You expect rejection and often reject others first in order to avoid anticipated pain.
- You may avoid relationships altogether, believing you are better off controlling your environment.
- You find regulating emotions difficult and often act impulsively, causing major ruptures in your relationships.
- You have a hard time developing trusting relationships though you value connection.
- You feel like life is "happening to you."
- You are uncomfortable working toward any sort of challenge or risk.
- You struggle staying focused.
- You may struggle with mental health issues or addiction.[3]

Again, there's hope. Your attachment style can shift based on the stability and loving care found in future relationships.

Disorganized Relationship with God

Sara had a bipolar father. On the one hand, he was brilliant. He would often make her feel special and encourage her gifts. On the other hand, he raged and was emotionally abusive. His cutting sarcasm became the voice of her inner critic, even as an adult. Once, she watched him throw her mother down stairs. When I asked how her story translated to her relationship with God, Sara said, "I never doubted that God loves me. I was a daddy's girl and I felt special to God. However, just like with my dad, I'm not sure He can be trusted completely. I have learned to rely on myself."

For twenty-five years, Sara's husband has been incredibly even-tempered and loving, but even in that relationship, Sara "reads the room" before determining how much to share about her own needs. She still feels like she has to be self-reliant.

Fear hinders healthy attachment. When our world is colored by fear, or at least by confusion, we are left wandering without a map. We scan every room and every relationship for a predator. It's the same in our relationship with God. Can we receive attunement and comfort from the One we're unconsciously scooting away from?

How We're Taught to Fear God

Because fear has been used as a tool for transformation in so many churches, an insecure disorganized attachment with God may be even more prevalent than an insecure disorganized attachment with your primary caregiver. Why? You may have been introduced to the Christian life by churches that described a god who was scary, confusing, or bizarre. Maybe you came from a background where fear was induced on purpose. Instead of translating "the *fear* of the LORD is the beginning of wisdom" (Prov. 9:10) as holy awe, you were given reason to expect God's presence was capricious at best, and at worst, a pot of rage always ready to boil over. You were taught there were a hundred things that could fit onto this blank line: "If you don't do _____ and you die, you'll experience the full weight of the wrath of God."

Fear was used as a way to keep your behavior or your belief systems in line. Perhaps fear was even used to pave the way for evangelism, but fear can never be used as an inducement to attachment. If fear is introduced before trust is built, you will always have your guard up. Rest requires internal safety. At best, we will keep God at a safe distance and serve Him to keep Him happy, marking His moods and wondering how we can stay on His "good side."

If you've struggled to feel a desire to be present with God, this might be why. If God has seemed scary, confusing, or bizarre, think about the child in the Strange Situation as their mother walked into the room. They assessed their felt sense of safety and asked themself, *Should I ignore her and keep playing with my toys? Should I go toward her and risk abuse? Maybe if I give her a display of submission, I'll be pleasing to her.* Perhaps you're not sure you want to experience God present. *Is He safe?* you wonder.

Peter, James, and John had witnessed Jesus do exorcisms, heal the sick, and free captives. They were there when God's voice echoed above His Son at His baptism: "This is my Son, whom I love; with him I am well pleased" (Matt. 3:17). When Jesus blazed like light at the transfiguration, conversing with Moses and Elijah, they were there (Matt. 17:1–3). Daily, they shared meals with the Alpha and Omega, the One who calms storms and speaks solar systems into existence. Yet, at the Last Supper, John felt so safe that he laid his head on Jesus's chest. He had experienced enough of God's goodness that even though Jesus was completely other, he knew the safest place on earth was in Emmanuel's presence. The safest place on earth was together.

What Safety Feels Like

If you have an insecure disorganized attachment, you were probably left alone to contend with your fear as a child. You had no one to hold the fury of your stifled anger or make sense of your perplexing story.

You were left alone, and unfortunately, because of your unstable or alarming caregiver, alone was safer than together.

This was not your fault. This was what safety felt like. It was what you needed to do to survive. But this hiding isn't serving you well anymore. It's time to let safe people in. And when you're ready, it's time to let God in. It's time to be together because together is where healing begins.

First, crawl into the arms of God. Maybe you've seen Andrei Rublev's icon of the Holy Trinity, which shows three angelic beings around a table, their heads inclined toward each other. They look peaceful, connected, content. The icon is also called *The Hospitality of Abraham*. Remember the three beings who travel to see Abraham and tell him of the promised child, Isaac, in Genesis 18? In early Christian thought, the three beings who visited Abraham were the Trinity.

In 2016, a five-year-old boy from Aleppo was pulled from the wreckage of an airstrike. He was bloody, dusty, and grey. While sitting in a busy hospital, he became the symbol of the horror of the war in Syria. On Facebook, this little boy's image was photoshopped and instead of sitting on the orange chair in the hospital, he was surrounded by the wings of the Holy Trinity in Rublev's icon. It was a visual prayer for all the innocents of Syria. This child, covered with the terror of war, was standing in. He was still bloodied, but he was now surrounded by Father, Son, and Holy Spirit. He was still hurting, but healing was at hand.

Your young and hurting parts are always welcome into the very heart of God. David penned, "You have surrounded me *on every side*, behind me and before me, and You have placed Your hand *gently* on my *shoulder*" (Ps. 139:5 Voice).

Eventually, the Father, Son, and Holy Spirit will become your shield, your Healer, and the Redeemer of your story. You may have to experience this profound presence through the hands of kind people first. Let them position you in the presence of the Trinity. Look for a safe therapist, a spiritual director, or a small group that can hold your story with you.

Second, let God the Father join you, even in your distancing. There was a couple who had been waiting for an adoption for years. It had taken time, finances, and focus, but finally a six-year-old boy was coming home with them. As they planned their first dinner together, the mother made macaroni and cheese, chicken nuggets, pizza, *and* peanut butter and jelly sandwiches. She didn't know her son's favorites yet and decided to give him a smorgasbord of options all on one plate.

Finally, he was sitting at their table with them. The new mother and father kept beaming at their child and at each other, cherishing the fact that at last their little boy was at their table. It was at this moment that the boy grabbed his plate, left the utensils on the table, pushed away from the table, climbed out of his seat, and set the full plate on the floor. For a moment the mother and father were stunned as they watched the boy use his hands to shove as much food as possible into his mouth. Then the father pushed his own chair away from the table, took his own plate, and placed it on the floor to join his little boy.[4]

You may feel like avoiding God, like stiff-arming the presence to keep Him safely out of view, but He welcomes every opportunity to join you where you are.

Just know, it's okay if you can't do the practices described in the second half of this book. The information may feel overwhelming, and you may have to set it down and come back to it later. Be patient with yourself. Find safe people to slowly walk you into the warm embrace of His lavish love.[5]

Visit summerjoygross.com/the-emmanuel-promise to access a video of a quiet Lectio Divina of Psalm 139:5.

5

Becoming Securely Attached

After learning about attachment wounds, we can feel a bit raw. Maybe this is new information. Maybe it's not. When I first discovered how many areas of my life my attachment wound affected, I was distraught. I remember chatting with my mom on the phone during one particular walk around my neighborhood. "I'm insecure anxious, Mom. I keep butting my head against these ingrained behaviors." My marriage was suffering from my fear of abandonment. My friendships were suffering from a fear of rejection. I was getting stuck in patterns of rumination. My relationship with God was suffering as I pendulumed between my need for validation and my desire to numb. Anxiety and hypervigilance patterns were carved into my nervous system and needed to be managed almost daily.

I tell you these things to show you that I've been there. And here's the good news. Our brains were designed with the possibility for transformation written right into the code, and the Holy Spirit has the key. Maybe you're wondering if it's too late to change, and you wish this information had landed in your lap decades earlier. If this is you, I hope you'll see this entire book as a gentle invitation. No matter where you are on the journey, Emmanuel is reaching out. Can you see His eyes shining toward you, His hand outstretched?

You don't have to fight toward healing alone. Can you hear Him whispering, "We are in this together"? And don't you think *together* is the loveliest word in the English language?

Your Emmanuel loves the word *come*: "Come to Me and you will find rest. Come eat with Me. Come, all who are thirsty. Come dwell with Me. Come abide with Me. Come attach to Me. Let Me become your home." There's no time stamp on these invitations. Let's start now.

The fact that the human brain can continue to change even in adulthood was only accepted by neuroscientists twenty to twenty-five years ago. The concept is called neuroplasticity, plasticity meaning moldable. It's important to remember that God designed the brain. None of this is new to Him. Science is just catching up with the truth Paul proclaimed in Romans 12:2. Our brains *can* be renewed.

We rewire our brains through one powerful encounter with God after another until we can return often, safe in the refuge of His arms. Attachment researchers call this new, strong bond an earned secure attachment, an awkward phrase for Christians. We do not *earn* God's love, *earn* grace, or *earn* adoption as a child of God. They are all costly gifts from God as a result of His lavish love and the power of the cross. As we accept this unearned grace, our adoption is sealed.

Perhaps we can see earned secure attachment as a process of earned trust. Is God worthy of our trust? Of course He is. Yet, trust that transforms our sense of security takes time to establish, and *this* is the goal in receiving God's invitation to attachment. Our brains are renewed as we fall back into the arms of God over and over and trust our Emmanuel is always available and care is always at hand. This is the Emmanuel promise.

We've looked at insecure attachment styles, but what are the marks of a person with a secure attachment? A child with an earned secure attachment has a sense that their needs are welcome, and they have an intuitive pattern of refuge-seeking and exploration.

The Secure Child

For ten years, my husband and I pastored a church in South Haven, Michigan—Priscilla and Aquila style, passing babies back and forth between the sermon and the announcements. All three of our children were born right there in the village hospital. We loved our town.

The grass of the city block–sized park on the bluff in South Haven runs nearly up to Lake Michigan. You can watch kids on the monkey bars and turn and see a white sailboat catch a breeze beside the red, metal lighthouse. We lived where others vacationed.

Our little yellow cottage was just five blocks away from the park. On summer afternoons, I piled the kids into the stroller. Maddie rode in back, standing on a step stool, just peeking over the orange umbrella. Caedmon dribbled a soccer ball beside us, learning to anticipate the sidewalk's uneven folds with every bounce. Xavier sat in front in a blue Superman shirt borrowed from a pajama ensemble, a red cape Velcroed to the shoulders.

As soon as we arrived and parked the stroller, Maddie and Caedmon ran off to visit their favorite sections of the wooden park. They are nineteen months apart—easy companions. Every once in a while, they returned for a juice box before running after newly made friends.

But Xavier's big blue eyes never strayed from my gaze for long. The more attached a child is at that age, the more they will keep their caregiver in view. As he climbed steps and slid down slides, his Superman cape flying, he glanced up as if asking, "Did you see that, Mom?" looking for my delight to match his. Occasionally, he came back for my hand, and I coached him over the balance beam or held him up to grasp the monkey bars. After a scrape, he buried his face in my shoulder, angry, frustrated, and hurt. I smelled his salty, sweaty head and held him close until he calmed down enough to sit on my lap, looking outwards. Eventually he grabbed a handful of Pepperidge Farm fish crackers I offered him. Then, comforted, he ventured off again.

No one had told him to discount his emotions or dismiss his needs or stop listening to the ups and downs of his nervous system. Children who are securely attached are intuitive in seeking care. Hungry? Run to mom. Frustrated? Run back to her arms to calm down. Relaxed and regulated, they venture forth to conquer. They experience comfort and care in the secure base of their mother's arms, venture out to explore, and then run back to security over and over as needed, searching for Mom's attentive gaze.

We see this same intuition to seek care clearly in Psalm 18:

> In my distress I called to the LORD;
> I cried to my God for help,
> From his temple *he heard my voice*;
> my cry came before him, into his ears. (v. 6, emphasis added)

> He reached down from on high and took hold of me;
> he drew me out of deep waters. (v. 16)

> He brought me out into a spacious place;
> he rescued me because he delighted in me. (v. 19)

Later in the chapter, after David rests in God's delight, he once again feels empowered and ready to explore.

> It is God who arms me with strength
> and keeps my way secure.
> He makes my feet like the feet of a deer;
> he causes me to stand on the heights. . . .
> You provide a broad path for my feet,
> so that my ankles do not give way. (vv. 32–33, 36)

Somewhere along the road, we stopped listening to our bodies' basic messages. We learned to grit it out and turn off the messages of our healthy needs. We stopped crying out. We learned which emotions were acceptable to our caregivers and earned comfort and which ones we needed to drop from our repertoire. Unfortunately, this sifting ended up creating little caricatures of our true selves. We became either people pleasers who were more in tune with our parents' inner world than our own or children who stopped listening to our needs altogether. We stopped running to parental arms for comfort.

Listening to our bodies' messages becomes part of our journey to secure attachment to God. It is an invitation to become childlike. Listen to the words of Emmanuel: "Unless you change and become like little children, you will never enter the kingdom of heaven" (Matt. 18:3). We need to become guileless again.

In order to develop an earned secure attachment, we start by relearning our instincts and listening to our needs. Please note that I didn't say obeying our instincts. We listen and come, allowing God to discern them with us.

During childbirth classes, my classmates and I were shown a video of a newborn, fresh out of the womb's comforting darkness and laid on the mother's belly. She was a naked elf-looking creature with a misshapen head, who inched toward the smell of milk. No one had taught her to search for milk at a breast. Searching for nurture is instinctual. You, too, have needs woven into the framework of your brain in order to keep you moving toward care. Your needs are invitations to seek safety and connection.

That same baby will look into the eyes of her mother's adoring gaze. You can watch it fill the infant up. Six to eight weeks later, as she receives the gaze of the mother, delight washes over her and she slowly begins to embody joy. Her limbs start kicking, and she breaks out into a smile. The newborn receives the attentive gaze of her mother with her entire body.

Many of us struggle just to recognize our need. Even the idea of having a need may give us a rash. Our attachment wound has taught us there's no one to depend on, but in order to be open to a new attachment to our Abba, recognizing need and turning toward

Monday Morning Practical: Tuning In

If listening to your body and becoming aware of your emotions feels awkward or uncomfortable, follow these steps:

1. Begin by reading the Psalms. Listen to David's and the other psalmists' emotions as they came up uncensored before the Lord. These raw emotions were not dismissed; they became part of the canon for worship. Their uncensored prayers became our prayers. Their crying out became an avenue for us to cry out. Stay in step 1 as long as needed.
2. Take time each day to check in on your emotions. Rate how you are feeling from 1 to 10. Great? Write down a number between 7 and 10. Not great? Write down a number between 1 and 3.
3. Use a feeling wheel and ask yourself, How am I feeling? (Note: You are rarely one thing at a time.)
4. Do a body scan slowly from the top of your head to your toes. Note where you're holding joy and energy. Note where you are holding tension. Is there a story there? What does that energy or tension tell you about the story that you are presently in?
5. Follow David's lead by writing a lament. Tell God how you're feeling. Use details. What has the lament cost? Emotionally? Physically? Spiritually? Relationally?
6. Read your lament to a safe person.

Him is our first step. David describes this cry and response in Psalm 40:1–2. I adore the image of God's ear inclined to His son:

> I waited patiently for the LORD;
>> he inclined to me and heard my cry.
> He drew me up from the pit of destruction,
>> out of the miry bog,
> and set my feet upon a rock,
>> making my steps secure. (ESV)

Dear One, can you see God's ear "inclined to" you? He is always attentive, tenderly watchful, and never too busy to listen, whether it's a deep heart cry or just a ramble through your day. Those whose caregivers were not "tuned in" may struggle to experience this beautiful call and response with God. Sometimes life demands every ounce of attention we have, and we don't recognize the attentiveness of God until we look back and see His faithfulness dotted through the chapters of our autobiography. This, too, builds trust.

Others of us struggle with emotions that are so big, we find ourselves fighting the chaos before crying out or trying to understand it by ruminating. The emotional chaos is sometimes amorphous, or what I call a "generalized feeling of yuck." Maybe you recognize that feeling too? It's hard to cry out when we don't know what our cry consists of. We spend all our time trying to untangle the knots. We ask, *Lord, would You brood over the chaos of thoughts and feelings? Would You show me what to pay attention to? Would You help me discern the true cry of my heart?*

This is the invitation. Our Emmanuel, present with us now, desires to hear the cry of our heart. "What do you want Me to do for you?" He asks. The beauty of this exchange is that we are turning our face toward His, recognizing His ability to meet our need. When

A Prayer Exercise for Bringing Our Heart's Cry to God

Take a few deep breaths and place your right hand on your heart. Pay attention to the senses in the room. What do you hear? What temperature do you feel? What do you see?

With your eyes closed, picture Jesus with His hands outstretched to you in invitation. He's asking you the question, What do you want Me to do for you? (Mark 10:51). Allow the deep cry of your heart to respond, and then share that desire with Him.

we turn toward the gaze of our Emmanuel, carrying forward our heaviness for Him to make sense of and heal, He calls this faith.

The 6 Needs Compass of Connection

Dr. Jeffrey Olrick, a clinical psychologist who works as an attachment specialist, wrote the book *The 6 Needs of Every Child* with his wife and coauthor, Amy Olrick. The principles about attachment in that book give us a glimpse into different categories of need for an earned secure attachment to be created. The secure child has more than one need. According to Jeffrey Olrick, they have six. These translate beautifully into our relationship with our Abba.

What do we need to form a secure attachment? We need delight, support, and boundaries as well as equipping, comfort, and protection.[1]

The Olricks made this simple for us to envision with their compass of needs. It's divided brilliantly into two categories: (1) draw near (or refuge-seeking) and (2) exploration.

Remember the illustration of my son Xavier playing on the playground, running off to explore and then running back to seek comfort and a secure base in my arms? This represents both the refuge-seeking and the exploration points of the Olricks' compass.

What you didn't hear is that because Xavier was so young, I gave him *boundaries*. "You can play on this slide, but unless I'm directly underneath you, you can't use the zip line." I watched him, and as he got close to the rope net, I stood underneath so he didn't fall without arms to gather him. My presence was his *protection*. I held his hand as he walked across the balance beam, *equipping* him. "Hey, buddy," I said, "see how it feels to hold your arms out for extra balance. Now, heal to toe, heal to toe, like this." Then I gave him my hand as he walked across his first few times, *supporting* him.

In *The 6 Needs of Every Child*, the Olricks teach,

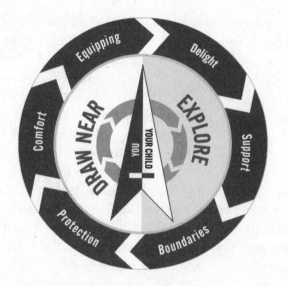

Taken from *The 6 Needs of Every Child* by Amy Elizabeth Olrick and Jeffrey Olrick, PhD. Copyright © 2020 by Amy Olrick and Jeffrey Olrick. Used by permission of HarperCollins Christian Publishing.

Three needs make up the "Explore," or exploration, side of the compass:

Delight: I see you! Discovering and expressing your love.

Support: How can I help? Anticipating opportunities and obstacles.

Boundaries: How far is too far? Defining and valuing limits.

Three needs make up the "Draw Near," or refuge-seeking, side of the compass:

Protection: Are you safe? Resolving to protect from true harm.

Comfort: I see your suffering. Moving close to ease the pain.

Equipping: Where to from here? Finding a way forward with hope and a plan.[2]

Patterns of Refuge-Seeking and Exploration

This pattern of drawing near and exploration can be seen in the way Jesus ministered with the band of men who followed Him. After keeping the disciples close and teaching them, one town at a time,

Jesus prepared to send them out on mission in Luke 10 by inviting them into His same Isaiah 61 ministry of healing, freeing, and restoring. But before sending them out, Jesus *equipped* them and gave them *boundaries* with notes such as these: Do not take extra money. A worker is worth his keep. Search for a worthy person and stay at their house. Then, interestingly enough, *He didn't go with them.* He equipped them, sent them out, and then stood on the sidelines watching them explore. My guess is that He also interceded on their behalf, providing *support* just as He provides for us now.[3]

After their missionary journey, they ran back to Him with stories. Scripture says that Jesus rejoiced [*egalliasato*], jumping up and down with them and praising God in delight (Luke 10:21). They had experienced the Father's wisdom and power. On their own! Just like a secure child on the playground, exploring and returning to home base in the heart of their caregiver, sometimes attachment with God looks similar. We establish a home base, allowing strength to build, going out to explore and create, to work and play, and then, once again, we draw near to the presence of God, reestablishing Him as our place of refuge.

We also see patterns of refuge-seeking, nourishment, and then exploration in the Liturgy of the Hours used in monasteries. The bell rings seven times a day, beckoning the monks back to the chapel for short services from before dawn to bedtime. Whether they're gardening, studying, or making that night's stew, as soon as they hear the bell, the monastics silently file into the chapel and slide into the wooden pews to chant the Psalms or have the eucharistic bread and wine. They draw near and are sent out to explore all day long.

Sometimes, as we create patterns for refuge-seeking and exploration, we schedule them. Morning prayer. Evening prayer. We follow a liturgy or just bracket a time of stillness to rest in God's presence. Or, like Xavier looking back at me, sharing a moment with a glance, refuge-seeking can be simple, a quick embrace with a breath prayer. A piece of music can even give us five minutes to rest in the comfort of God's presence. Other times we wait for a longer period to process emotions, taking out our journal and having a conversation during a scheduled time of drawing near.

Be thoughtful with your day, your comings and goings. Experiment. Soak in God's love with your morning coffee, receive your identity as His beloved. Savor. Linger and let it inform your next few hours. Move out saturated with love. Before bed, reflect on your day. Ask God to reveal where He met you with His presence and provision, then crawl under the warmth of God's wing. Your presence, Dear One, is the longing of His heart.

Life comes at you hard. Build rhythms of attachment on the easy days so you can encounter the comfort of your Emmanuel on the hard days. Choose from the list of practices in the second half of the book. Listen to the Spirit's invitation. These become the rhythms of those receiving an earned secure attachment.

Ready to put this into practice? Push play on the videos for this chapter's Monday Morning Practical, "The Prayer Exercise for Bringing Your Heart's Cry to God," and a Lectio Divina on Psalm 40:1–2 at summerjoygross.com/the-emmanuel-promise.

6

Dark Night of the Soul

Sometimes the spiritual life feels more like a wrestling than an invitation to an embrace. It feels more like the story of Jacob in hand-to-hand combat than the glorious vision of the angels ascending and descending the ladder to heaven.[1] Just remember—both of these experiences happened to the same person. It may seem like a contradiction, but it's a clear picture of the uncomfortable dissonance in most of our spiritual journeys. But dissonance, dear friends, can lead us straight into the arms of God even though we're wrestling. The question is, Will we continue wrestling through the night, inviting God into our doubts and pain, holding on until the blessing is given, or will we walk away?

Dear One, what if God is inviting you to bring Him your fiercest battle? He desires you to place the full power of your inner storm in His waiting arms. He prefers your authentic engagement over your limp assent.

How does it feel to know that He wants you to bring up the internal battle that's boring a hole in your stomach, to unleash the questions you've been denying, and to dig up your disappointments on how your life has turned out? How does it feel to know He wants you to thrust *all the pain* into His capable arms?

Because, Dear One, this invitation to wrestle is actually an invitation to intimacy. This may feel impossible to believe since these seasons of internal wrestling are often accompanied by a sense that God's nearness is being withheld.[2]

Let's talk about this for a moment. First, can I just say that although we may not sense God's presence, that doesn't change the truth that He is here. As C. S. Lewis wrote, "God's presence is not the same as the feeling of God's presence and He may be doing most for us when we think He is doing least."[3] Both a sense of the presence as well as the desire that is intensified by a sense of absence can be part of His invitation.

Classically, this season of spiritual depression is called the Dark Night of the Soul. The Dark Night can feel like doubt, confusion, anger, disappointment, grief, discouragement, or even despair. These are the cries that arise from our most tender stories and, with David, we cry out, "How long, LORD? Will you forget me forever? How long will you hide your face from me? How long must I wrestle with my thoughts and day after day have sorrow in my heart? . . . Give light to my eyes, or I will sleep in death" (Ps. 13:1–3).

The truth is that although we may feel abandoned, we are drawn tight against the warm breast of God, even when we're in the pitch black and we're disoriented. We may have spiritual vertigo. But could this disorientation be necessary?

In the Dark Night, the map of the comfortable Christian life suddenly ends, like the medieval maps of the earth that pointed to the edge of the parchment with these words: "Here be dragons." It's in the darkness, in the disorientation, and in the disillusionment that, like Eustace in *The Voyage of the Dawn Treader*, we are undragoned. In the Dark Night, we are being made stronger, humbler, and a whole lot more tender.

As I think of the Dark Night of the Soul, I hear this Haggai Scripture from the libretto from Handel's *Messiah*: "Thus saith the LORD of hosts; Yet once, it is a little while, and I will shake the heavens, and the earth, and the sea, and the dry land; and I will shake all nations, *and the desire of all nations shall come*" (2:6–7 KJV, emphasis added).

85

Seeking Companionship in the Darkness

When we're in the Dark Night, we don't know how long the shaking will take. Will there be aftershocks? We wonder if anything will be standing afterward. Our assumptions about the Christian life are shaken. Formulas make way for mystery. Self-mastery makes way for surrender. Our image of God Himself is shaken. We thought we knew exactly who we were dealing with, but during our Dark Night, we realized that we had a tight grip on an artificial idol. We did not give Him the ability to reveal Himself to us. We did not surrender to the true God.

After the pandemic, many of us have been in a season of shaking. And here's what I wonder, Will we invite God into our doubts and pain, or will we find it easier to walk away? If you are going through an internal shaking, can I invite you to search out and hold on to those solid people you've found on the Christian journey, people who will walk with you with kindness and not ego, with patience and not fear? Companionship in the Dark Night provides the courage we need to wait until the blessing is revealed in the first light of morning.

Many of the Dark Nights I've witnessed with friends and directees started with the unraveling of formulas as someone approached midlife. The if/then statements they built their life on no longer held when their spouse got cancer, their child struggled with depression, or they were invited into the boss's office on a Friday afternoon to hear that their job had been eliminated. In frustration, some decided that God was not as powerful as they were taught. Others threw it all away, believing that the preachers they listened to could no longer be trusted.

Sometimes this if/then formula is preached from the pulpit. We can even find it in Scripture: "Keep this Book of the Law always on your lips; meditate on it day and night, so that you may be careful to do everything written in it. Then you will be prosperous and successful" (Josh. 1:8).

Somewhere along the way, we've married the American dream with what God meant by "prosperous," and it makes me wonder how Paul, beaten, bruised, and chained, preached the book of Joshua. I wonder how he defined success. I wonder how Jesus, bruised and crushed by our iniquities, measured "blessing." Suffering is a part of the human experience. Always has been since the fall.

For years, though, I believed suffering was for people who didn't get the formula right. Then I had to reckon with the story of my own abuse. It wasn't until years later, after I had done extensive healing work with my therapist, that this thought kept popping up, *I wasn't protected. I did everything right, and God didn't hold up His side of the bargain. Didn't He promise protection?* I had firmly believed the formula: We do for God and He shelters us from suffering. After the abuse I experienced, I started questioning everything about God. These two questions were at the heart of my wrestling—Is He good? and Is He powerful?

Constructive wrestling requires good companions. In Switzerland there's a handful of chalets just up the mountain from Lake Lucerne called L'Abri, which when translated from French means "the shelter." Francis Schaeffer thought he was moving to Switzerland to become a missionary for French-speaking Swiss, but instead, he ended up opening his home to wanderers wrestling with their faith. After college, my husband and I trekked up the mountain and stayed for four months.

At L'Abri, I found tutors who held my hand through the darkness. My questions did not surprise them, scare them, or make them shrink back. They were my first spiritual directors. It was there in Switzerland that I learned to lament and bring the depth of my anger to the feet of Jesus. I raged. I wrestled. I asked God, "Where were you?"

The Dark Night finally ended as I was ready to allow God to reveal Himself to me, no strings attached. Philosopher Miguel de Unamuno wrote, "Those who believe they believe in God, but without passion in the heart, without anguish of mind, without uncertainty, without doubt, and even at times without despair, believe only in the idea of God, and not in God himself."[4]

The Gifts of the Dark Night

In the wrestling of the Dark Night, ego and self-assuredness are stripped. Everything we have been using to control our world has experienced a shaking. For most, the darkness reveals the cracks in our image of God and the way we've coddled our false ego. In suffering, our pride is dismantled brick by brick.

As our titles are stripped, we find we are blessed to be a child of God, no more, no less. We are no longer naming ourselves; we are named by Another. We find we are in the school of love. We become open to relationship with the Father, Son, and Holy Spirit, not using Him for our ends, but ready for a new type of cruciform surrender. We become softer, more compassionate.

Our job? Keep wrestling. Paying attention to your questions is brave. Don't be afraid of doubt. Doubt can be the doorway to a deeper faith. Dear One, He can handle it. He's big enough to hold it all.

Finally, I want to encourage you to keep wrestling with your face turned *toward* God. Part of our ultimate healing is allowing every doubt, each "Where were you?" and every "If only you had been there"[5] to rise up before Him. We stay in the ring *with* God, even through the hot tears, the disappointments, and the dismantling.

In our wrestling, we feel His compassion. He knows what the questions have cost. He understands the suffering that has led us to this point. We sense Jesus, our Emmanuel, the same One who cried out in Gethsemane, drawing near with compassion. Refusing to leave. Holding us. Loving us through the weeping. Eventually, the One we wrestle with becomes the One whose arms we rest in. Eventually, the dawn comes, and we receive a new blessing, a new name, and the invitation to a new vocation.

Maybe you remember a season of wrestling. Maybe you don't. Go to summerjoygross.com/the-emmanuel-promise to access a Lectio Divina of Jacob wrestling with the angel.

7

A Doorway for Connection

One Christmas Eve in Philly when I was home from college, my family drove to a big-box megachurch at dusk. We were new in town. Gone were the long-cultivated traditions like sleeping by the fire in our sunken living room, Dad sneaking in during the night to add more logs to the fire and use the billows. Gone was walking through the church door to be greeted by warm smiles, unwrapping layer by layer of winter clothes, setting boots under the coatrack, and exchanging them for "church shoes." Gone was the joy of being invited up onstage to sing and lead. Gone was the feeling that I knew my place.

After I packed the van and headed to college, my family moved nine hours away from Northern Ohio. I needed a MapQuest printout to find my way back to my people over the holidays. I had left home and there was no going back.

I'm sure they sang carols in the megachurch. There were probably Christmas trees with white lights and an orchestra with a full horn section, but those details have slipped my memory. It was on the drive home in the darkness to our new apartment that Christmas began. On the left and right of us, whole neighborhoods were lit with luminaria, white paper bags filled with sand and a small votive candle. Every ten feet a new bag perforated the darkness around cul-de-sacs and curving roads. We drove through one neighborhood after another, hushed by the beauty of warm light bouncing off the snow.

Sometimes God's presence is like that. We're sojourning in a new land like Jacob and are surprised to see where God shows up.

"Surely the LORD is in this place, and I was not aware of it," Jacob said after seeing the vision of angels ascending and descending the ladder to heaven (Gen. 28:16).

Other times God extends an invitation for us to cultivate a close walk with Him through the liminal places of our lives, one moment to another, the darkness punctuated by the light of His presence.

So here's my question: Is it possible to intentionally place sensory reminders of the truth of God's presence and walk from present moment to present moment using them to remind us that God is here, whether it is a lit candle, a praise song on repeat, the liturgy of the hours, or a cross in your pocket?

Presence Candle

The presence candle was lit on my kitchen island that morning. It has become a part of my morning ritual. I need a flaming bush, a reminder that every moment is filled with God, every moment is holy. Every once in a while, I looked up from the computer to watch the flame flicker, remembering in the midst of my everyday-ordinary, "God, You are here." The kids filled the dishwasher after last night's burgers but left a sink full of the big pans. The iron was still out from Sunday morning's rush, and the chai tea I'd been sipping since my first son got up for school at six was waiting for a refill. This was my ordinary semi-controlled chaos. It was not cleaned-up-perfect. It was not scrubbed. Yet God was in it, even in the midst of my mess, and the flicker of the candle reminded me to look for Him.

While speeding through my day, I needed a still point, like the clock on the wall that dancers keep returning to as they accomplish their turns. An anchor. This candle called me back, reminding me of the truth: I am never outside the warmth of God's love.

It also reminded me that His presence does not depend on my awareness. The flicker does not stop the moment I forget it's there. The candle keeps burning, whether my awareness is turned in its direction or not. In the same way, God does not disappear as my attention strays elsewhere, though I may function as if that's the case.

And here's the brain science around this practice of keeping a lit candle in a common space: by using a constant reminder of God's presence, we're laying the groundwork for *spiritual object constancy*. Object constancy is the concept of believing that an object still has reality even when it's out of sight. As we build attachment to others, emotional object constancy is established. Even when that loved one is out of sight, we still have the internal security of our bond.

Our brains have been wired to scarcity, to absence, to loss. Sometimes our brains, through loss, have been wired to believe we will be abandoned. Lavish love is a new landscape we need a map to find. But just having the map is not enough. We have to travel the road until we can consistently find our way home. Our brains need to be rewired for perfect love.

As I click on the butane lighter or strike the match, I speak this simple prayer, "You are here,"[1] and the lit flame awakens me to God's nearness. I come awake to the fact that God has already declared Himself present.

Building Security through Object Constancy

At ten years old, Sofia refused to sleep when she was brought home to the States from the African orphanage. Every night was a battle. Her adopted mother followed all the conventional advice, establishing a slow bedtime routine—bath, books, time for cuddling. But as soon as her mother walked out the door, Sofia panicked. If Sofia happened to fall asleep from exhaustion while her mom was still in the room, she woke up multiple times throughout the night reaching out frantically for her mom's presence. Her mother, Diana, finally figured out that Sofia equated her lack of presence with abandonment. For Sofia, abandonment was not a future fear but a reality she had experienced already. Her subconscious would not find quiet until the story had changed, and transforming a story takes time. The trauma inside Sofia's body told her to grasp, to hold, to not let go because it might all go "poof" in the darkness. Trust is built one marked experience of care after another. Sofia, of course, hadn't reached *emotional object constancy*. It takes time to establish that love is not scarce. It takes time to trust that love will be there tomorrow and the next day and the next. Again, emotional object constancy means a child believes love is present even when their caregiver has walked out of the room.

Have you ever played hide-and-seek with a toddler and watched them crawl out of the room looking for you when you were still sitting on the couch, a large mound covered with a blanket? When you pulled that blanket over your head, the little one no longer believed you were present. They had not yet achieved object permanence.

Until we achieve emotional object constancy, our internal sense of security is determined by the stories inked into our past, not the truth of the present.

It takes thousands of interactions of faithful loving care for a child to achieve emotional object constancy. Each time a caregiver responds consistently to a cry, each soothing voice, each nighttime rocking, each focus of delight gets stored in the brain and builds a neural pathway that creates a sense of security. Object constancy is transferred through the senses. We *feel* arms wrapped around us. We *see* eyes of love. We *hear* the soothing voice of the caregiver. We *smell* their skin. We *taste* milk.

Over time, the love of the caregiver is stored up within the child, and the child is given a sense that they are living in a safe and secure world. The child trusts the caregiver will continue to provide loving care.

Sofia's mom, aching from exhaustion, called her adoption services representative, and they had an idea. They suggested that Diana prove that she was still thinking about her daughter throughout the night and show her daughter that she was safe. So Diana strung a wire above Sofia's bed, and throughout the evening and occasionally at night, she would sneak into the room and clip a small, pink construction paper heart onto the wire. When Sofia woke up, she could visually see that she had not been abandoned, that her mom was thinking loving thoughts toward her during their separation. Love was still a reality, a visual reality. After a few weeks of pinning hearts, Sofia was able to sleep through the night peacefully. Sofia's trust grew night after night with the visual reminders of her mother's presence strung up one pink construction paper heart at a time.

Author Dr. Henry Cloud wrote this: "In the same way that a child develops emotional object constancy," we develop "spiritual object constancy."[2] When we are born again, spiritually speaking, we begin internalizing memories of God.

Dr. Cloud goes on, "It is refreshing to hear the writers of the Bible continually reminding the people to 'remember' when God did such and such, when he led them from here to there, or when he delivered them from such and such an enemy. God calls on our memory of spiritual experiences to give us courage to go further with him. We build a sense of 'spiritual object constancy' with God over the years as we log memories of trusting Him."[3]

God's Word Made Visible

After I graduated from Asbury College in December 1998, my husband, Andrew, and I had a large question mark on our calendar. Andrew wouldn't transfer to Calvin College's philosophy department until the next fall. As a graduation gift, my parents gave us a semester at L'Abri in Switzerland. There are a handful of L'Abri retreat centers around the world, and they are safe places to ask hard questions.

We were the only married students and were provided with a basement room in the central five-story chalet. Every morning as I pulled open the half curtains on our one small window, I gasped. There they were again: four peaks covered with snow, luminescent in the morning sun.

Andrew and I had met in high school in northern Ohio. I drove south from the flat cornfields around Norwalk. He drove north from the rolling hills of Amish country. School was in the middle. In comparison to home, the rugged Alps of Switzerland were a complete revelation. They were awe-inspiring. Looming. Stalwart.

Throughout my daily schedule, those four snow-covered peaks surprised me with a flash of brilliance, like a flashbulb going off on picture day. At breakfast, as we buttered slabs of still-warm bread, they were there. As I walked outside to shake out a rug during my chores, I gasped at the sight of them. When I sat listening to a tutor next to the pruned and dormant geraniums, the peaks were framed by the windows. Jim Ingram was the head of Swiss L'Abri, and every Sunday evening, we gathered around a lit fire as he read a chapter from one of C. S. Lewis's Narnia books. When we emerged from the fireplace room at his chalet, the snow-covered peaks glowed, keeping us company as we walked home.

I began to orient my sense of direction to their presence.

I went to L'Abri weary of wrestling. The problem of evil, the existence of evil in the presence of a loving God, wasn't just an intellectual puzzle in a dusty philosophy book; it was personal. I didn't question the existence of God; I questioned whether God was good.

"Doubt is sin," was proclaimed from the pulpit at Asbury during my time there. I squinted at the speaker. I already knew faith was on the other side of doubt, not in spite of it. I adored the school. I fell in love with learning with Dr. McKinley, who wore bow ties and sweater vests and taught world history as if letting us in on a grand secret. He pulled out a Ninja Turtle folder with his lecture tucked inside without cracking a grin. Dr. Vincent walked beside me as I explored words, and Dr. Brown introduced me to the craft of poetry in such a way that I have never completely recovered.

Asbury College was a safe place to explore becoming an adult but not a safe place to explore questions about God. I was given a book and a pat answer, and neither satisfied the level of trauma this question of God's goodness had erupted from.

I had been an innocent fourteen-year-old looking for safety and acceptance, and like many young girls, I sought belonging in a pair of male eyes. I found it in a leader in the youth group, but he was nineteen and I was not the first he had groomed. After those six months of abuse, Sunday school lessons about a God who protects His children rang hollow, and conversations about God being in control left me surly. How could it be that God was good when thousands of Thai were left dead on the beach from a tsunami, when the *Challenger* shuttle framed in the black-and-white TV of our fifth-grade classroom exploded, and when famine in the horn of Africa continued to shrink the next generation? How could God be good when I looked for someone to cherish me and instead found someone who was looking for easy prey?

At L'Abri, I was companioned on the journey, never handed a sticky note with a three-sentence answer from a Josh McDowell book. My wrestling was never preempted by someone else's certainty. I was given space to grieve, to occasionally beat my fists against God's chest, and then to find rest, the final blessing in the kindness of being heard. My questions did not embarrass, create a fight-or-flight reaction in the ears of my hearers, or make me feel pushed to the sidelines. My doubt was given hospitality. It was allowed to be transformed into faith at its own pace. I didn't know yet that faith in a good God would still take years to form. No one at L'Abri was trying to control my journey by pushing down on the fast-forward button.

Late that spring in Switzerland, a group of us brought an evening picnic uphill, poured a bottle of white wine between cups, and watched the full moon rise. It rose beside the four peaks, and the last of the spring snow nestled into the alpine valleys, shone bright, even at night, and I finally understood. The mountains were God's parable of presence. Those four peaks spoke a message of constancy. Solidity. Presence.

Every single morning as I pushed open the curtains, I would be awakened by this truth from Psalm 139: "When I awake, I am still with you" (v. 18).

Jesus often gleaned a message from the earth. Lilies of the field. Sparrows. A fig tree. Seeds growing in a field. He was listening to the Father's heart as it revealed itself in the world He had made. In sheep. In a vineyard. In ordinary bread, broken and blessed. For me, these mountains were a conduit of Emmanuel's presence made visible.

God of the Senses

Most of us move through our days without a felt sense of the presence of God. Of course we do. We're human. We are practical atheists, scrounging for love, or self-resilient, head down and barreling through a to-do list only to awaken to the presence in moments when our Bible is open or on Sunday mornings when a hymn surprises us awake. We walk through the world half asleep. And then it's as if the curtain is pulled back on the Holy of Holies, and we catch a glimpse of a larger mystery. *Oh yes*, we remember, *You are here*. His light perforates the darkness.

We long for a presence candle that's always lit, a reminder outside of ourselves. An ebenezer.

And it's completely understandable. We are a forgetful people, consumed with meeting our next need, sidestepping fear, checking off a to-do list, or listening to the loudest voice in the room. We require reminders, practices, whispers to remember to return home.

Throughout history, God provided object constancy through visuals of His presence. As He provided a way out of slavery, the presence of God in the Shekinah glory led the Israelites through the desert via a pillar of cloud by day and fire by night. The burning bush was on the move. As the Israelites looked at the fire glowing in the darkness, their worry was extinguished in His presence.

Listen to this verse tacked at the end of Exodus: "So the cloud of the LORD was over the tabernacle by day, and fire was in the cloud by night, *in the sight of all the Israelites during all their travels*" (40:38, emphasis added).

As they looked toward the tabernacle, they saw the glow of presence. As they trudged through the scrub brush, the light preceded them. As they walked out of their tents in the morning, the cloud was there. As they collected manna on the ground and stood up, straightening their backs, they saw a visual representation of God who had not forgotten them. As they lived and loved and struggled, He was there. The Lord knew the people of Israel would need a constant reminder of His nearness in order to begin to build attachment.

Earned secure attachment is built first on the foundation of presence. We're sensory people. We experience the world through sight, sound, touch, scent, and taste. Our senses are windows of connection. We are an embodied people. We need a truth that is embodied. That's why Jesus came to earth, to put mud on eyes so His people could see, to turn tables over and scatter injustice, to offer His scars to be touched. The Emmanuel chose to become the Word embodied.

In Psalm 19:1, David looked toward the stars and wrote these words: "The heavens tell of the glory of God" (NASB). When the Shekinah cloud, heavy with His presence, filled the temple in 2 Chronicles 5, the priests couldn't even stand up. When the Light of the World was placed in a young girl, she felt him kick and jump and push at the walls of her womb. After He was born, He was held and nursed by Mary, and then Simeon lifted Him up after waiting day and night for the Messiah at the temple. "For my eyes have *seen* your salvation" (Luke 2:30, emphasis added). Simeon and then wizened Anna literally held the salvation of the world in their arms. Hope took on flesh. Later, Jesus gave us bread and wine to taste His presence, to let it roll around in our mouths, to warm us as it goes down, to remind us He is not vapor, not a ghost. His presence is still incarnated. The Bread of Life has not been minimized by the passage of time, a long decrescendo. He was present then. He is present now.

Then, in Acts, after Jesus's ascension, we were given the Holy Spirit, and there were tongues of fire resting on heads, each person literally a burning bush, the presence taking up residence inside us.

Practice Nearness

These days I live in the suburban sprawl spreading out around Atlanta. No rugged white peaks. I light the presence candle on my kitchen island and it surprises me awake. "You are here," I speak, whispering the prayer. And sometimes, that's it. Nothing more. Just assent. Other times the flicker awakens need, repentance, a heart turned back toward His heart after I've eaten at a table set by scarcity.

The candle flickers as my patience thins and my voice raises at my children. It surprises me awake to the incongruence. I take a deep breath and then soften. The candle flickers as I turn on the TV and wonder if I want this story, this vision, to live side by side with the presence of God. I flick the TV off, and the silence is filled with invitation.

When we're in that deep slumber, we believe in the lie of separation. We believe we're alone, placed on Earth to pickaxe our way through our days, grasping for provision, mining for love. We miss the truth that the God who made the universe is actively pursuing our hearts, carrying the cross on His shoulders along the Via Dolorosa, the route Jesus was forced to carry His cross, the way of love. He was dying for desire for us.

He has been fighting our separation from day one.

Your invitation is to look for a presence candle in a glass jar, light it in your kitchen, or carry it around your house as you begin to establish the truth of your Emmanuel's constant presence.[4] He is always near. He is always in the room turned toward you. Always. Building a sense of spiritual object constancy is the first step toward your attachment with God.

———

You can access the videos for this chapter anytime. Push play on two Lectio Divina videos at summerjoygross.com/the-emmanuel-promise of Psalm 139 and Hebrews 13:5 in the Amplified Version.

8

God's Desire for Your Nearness

During the first ten years of my life, Dad was training to be a surgeon. I was along for the ride from the very beginning. Mom said I came out with a mischievous smile and the IUD in my fist. But even though I was born during a New York blizzard, just fifteen months after their wedding, my parents never made me feel like I wasn't right on time.

Back then, medical schools trained surgeons the way the Navy trains SEALs. These days there are laws governing the amount of time a resident can be in the hospital each week. That was not the case in the eighties. In order to observe their residents' decision-making skills, medical schools created extreme conditions, speeding past forty hours and not slowing down until residents reached eighty or even one hundred. The Maine Medical Center owned a house down the block for residents. Often on Sundays, Mom would make a lasagna and drive my brother and me to the Gorham House while Dad was on call. He'd hold Mom by the shoulders and look into her eyes with pure gratefulness.

Marriages were cracked wide open under the stress and absence caused by medical training. Dad shared his desire to be a surgeon after Mom learned every chief resident in the hospital had been divorced during their training.

Day by day, Mom kept the family sewn together with a teacher's certificate and a found family of friends. In the summer, we pulled a red wagon full of shovels and pails and peanut butter and jelly sandwiches to the beach with neighbors. My brother and I jumped over the waves in the still-frigid water and dribbled wet sand ribbons on fragile castles, decorating the doors and windows with sea glass and scallop shells. Then Mom piled us into the car covered with sand and slid us into a warm bathtub, toweling us off and putting us down for afternoon naps. Rinse and repeat all summer long.

She loved fiercely, suturing the fabrics of our lives together. During those five years, Mom had two more kids and a dwindling bank account. Residents only made four hundred dollars a week, and my parents were determined not to go in debt. The Goodall small group, which met at Mary and Jerry Goodall's house just north of Portland, became family. Memories of their house somehow seem warmer than our own. Our house felt empty without Dad.

Dad tried his best. He was intentional in everything he did, even fatherhood. I remember him playing nonsense games with me in the living room while Mom made beef barley soup, the recipe right off the box. He was a dragon with my pink knitted cap pulled tight over his ears, bottle-thick glasses askew. He tried to catch me as I ran from the brown, floral couch to the rattan rocking chair, trying to avoid his arms. He caught me, swung me around, and nearly crushed my tiny ribs with his barrel chest as he told me how much he loved me.

Dad was the first in his family line to go to college. His main goal was to make a life for he and Mom. In his bones, he held the same drivenness of his grandfather Barnett, who crawled out of the coal mines of Eastern Kentucky, blinking at the sunlight. With his young bride, the red-haired Jennie, Barnett bought a foreclosed farm in midcentral Ohio during the Great Depression and made something out of nothing before selling it and buying another foreclosed farm.

As a child, I didn't understand that Dad was exhausted and fighting for our future, just two steps removed from a life of poverty. I didn't see the adults working to hold together the stitches of our lives.

On his weekend off, he may have been looking at me, but his brain was working out the surgery he would perform Monday morning, or thinking through what went wrong with Mrs. Smith last Thursday on the operating table, or considering how to find enough time to practice new suture knots on the kit that sat on the shelf in our linen closet.

That was when my fawn or people-pleasing trauma response was born. I was always taking Dad's temperature like a little codependent, stepping carefully when he was weary and short. I was desperate to get his attention by dancing in front of him or singing a new tune. Maybe there was a secret word that would make his eyes widen and turn toward me. Sometimes he laid his head on a pillow on my lap while I watched TV, then he'd fall into a deep sleep, his arms crossed on his chest, his body twitching in his sleep, adrenaline from the hundred-hour weeks still coursing through his body. I would rub his thick mahogany hair the way his mother had. Whenever I was in his presence, I slipped too easily into fight-or-flight mode, sensitive to every whisper of turning away, of rejection. I was fighting for love. I was fighting to keep his eye on me. Dad's attention became an unattainable treasure.

Divine Attention

Imperfect human love has marred our brain's ability to receive love. We can't imagine a God who pursues us with unwavering desire.

We think we have to sing and dance for God, believing His attention is fleeting. We think we have to run after Him, waving our arms. We believe we have to follow formulas and memorize Scriptures as incantations in order to point His attention in our direction. We believe He will stay pleased with us and not slip away out of sight if we tick off a spiritual to-do list. We fear our secret sins will make Him stay hidden in a cosmic and crafty game of hide-and-seek. We are fearful that if we are found out, God will walk out and never come back.

Why would God be interested in the little girl in the mirror when people at the hospital were wavering between life and death? As a child, I couldn't imagine a God who longed for *my* presence.

Believing the lie of anthropomorphism—that God is a reflection of humans—I made God in the image of my father.

Psalm 139 disrupts all of my lies: "If I go up to the heavens, you are there; if I make my bed in the depths, you are there. . . . How precious to me are your thoughts, God! . . . Were I to count them, they would outnumber the grains of sand—when I awake, I am still with you" (vv. 8, 17, 18).

When I awake, I am still with you.

The God of Psalm 139 doesn't play hide-and-seek. He doesn't withhold His presence, demanding secret rites. He is not fickle or quick-tempered.

God doesn't weigh His attention on the balance of need. He doesn't have to. His attention is spacious. Limitless. He doesn't have the beeps and buzzes of a busy mind. He has ample time to stand with us as we gape at the wide smear in the sky that is the Milky Way, a thousand brilliant pinpoints. He has ample time to hold our hand and agree, "Yes, it is good." He leans over our shoulder as we cradle a newborn, wondering at the tiny bow of lips, the nearly translucent eyelids, and He whispers with joy in His voice, "Yes, she's very good." He sits on the couch, pulling us near as we watch the evening news, overwhelmed at the current of pain pulsing through the world.

He whispers as we create, provides wisdom as we work, walks beside us through the hospital where our mother is having surgery.

He holds hope while we hold only questions. As we limp through our days, wondering how the threads of our stories will find meaning, He holds together the disparate threads at the end of our story. The truth of God's omnipresence means He never has to choose one child over another. He never needs to check His phone for emergencies. He's present with each of His creations equally.

You have the full attention of the God of the universe.

God Has Ample Time for You

Sometimes God positions people in our life to give us a vision of the lavishness of His pace. He's not strangled by our calendar or handcuffed by our clocks. He is not racing against some human-determined finish line; our centuries are in the palm of His hand.

My Nona was a gardener with a flower bed in front of her picket fence, a riot of self-seeding color—purple columbine and bright red poppies snaking their heads toward the sun. Tiny violas lined the path, tangling and spilling onto the concrete.

They didn't behave. She didn't expect them to.

Gardeners have to be patient. They watch and nurture and wonder how much extra water is needed from the hose during an Ohio dry spell in August.

Nona used to laugh as she held out the hose for me to drink from when I was three or four and covered in watermelon juice, seeds stuck against my cheek. Somewhere in that backyard was an apple tree as old as Johnny Appleseed. Legend was that he had planted it. What a strange man, Johnny Appleseed, walking the northern Ohio roads with seeds in his pocket and a pan on his head. I wonder if he captured the imagination of following generations because of his eccentricity or because of his generosity. He seemed to be exceedingly generous with his time.

That's what we loved about my Nona too. She always seemed to have ample time. She was never in a rush. When I had sleepovers, Grandpa would begin banging pans, making breakfast before six, while Nona was still asleep. I'd crawl in bed with her, resting in the still-warm indentation his large body had left and pulling the covers up. Later, after Grandpa went to work, breakfasts were simple— eggs and toast with jam and tiny mismatched glasses filled with orange juice. We watched Regis and Kathy Lee and stayed in our nightgowns for hours.

Nona didn't need to be impressed. She didn't have to be fawned over; her love was a spacious one. Even as she was slipping into the darkness of Alzheimer's, she kissed me on the cheek, her peach fuzz–covered cheek against mine, and whispered, "I love you, sweetheart." She held that tender pose, one hand cradling my face. Those were the last words I ever heard her speak, and last words have a way of echoing down. Her love never ebbed and waned. It was never fickle or self-focused. It was contained, as if she was the sun and we were all looking up, warming ourselves.

You know that Bible verse in Revelation, the one where God is knocking on the door of your life? Dear One, the knocking never stops.

You are beloved on the days you walk easily through the world. You are beloved on the days you have fallen, with gravel embedded in your knees and palms. He longs to scoop you up, clean you off, and bring you home.

I always thought I had to clean myself up and make myself Sunday-morning-presentable to come into the presence of God. I believed His face was turned toward me only when I was on my best behavior.

Dear One, you are beloved in season and out.

Emmanuel is always knocking. Always available for connection. Always ready to light the fire, pour a cup of coffee, and hear how the world looks through your eyes, holding your heavy stories and watching as you pull up each joy and turn it over in your hand. It catches the light for a moment as you gaze together.

Right before His ascension, Jesus said this, "And surely I am with you always, to the very end of the age" (Matt. 28:20). These were His last words. And last words have a way of echoing down.

God-with-Us Initiates

I was the one who initiated, reaching for my future husband's hand on the bus as we traveled south from seeing *Phantom of the Opera* in Toronto. I was the pursuer. Why? Andrew didn't have the imagination for it. I was a senior. He was a sophomore. (Can you hear Andrew laughing twenty-seven years later? "Yeah, you grabbed my hair and dragged me into the cave." When he tells this story, it takes on a completely different tenor.)

But I had seen the respect he gave the hunched-over, silver-haired man, shaking the stranger's hand with both of his. We had toured Toronto as a high school singing group and were paired up at a microphone, tenor and soprano. Andrew kept us laughing as we mimicked Beach Boys dance moves while waiting for our sound guy to give us check-ins. I had seen him play with my younger siblings at a retreat, speaking to them in the same respectful tone he used for his uncles. The sparkle in his eyes was always genuine. The smell of his leather jacket spoke of earthy confidence.

He was surprised at the pursuit, confused even, but I had seen more wisdom and kindness in his character than in guys much older. But his disbelief meant I had to pursue him again and again until his questions were dispelled.

God's pursuit of Israel was constant. He was always the prime mover, the initiator, driven to bring His bride home. It is not in His nature to stop, to walk away, to abandon. Even when God allowed His people to be taken far from Him, their absence was an invitation. It was a beckoning to return.

All through history, God's eye has been set on dwelling with His people. And whenever we see a theme spread from Genesis through Revelation, we can be 100 percent positive that it's deep in the core of God's character.

At creation, He made us for Himself and invited Adam and Eve to walk with Him in the cool of the day. I love the idea of an evening walk with God after the gardening tools have been cleaned and set aside. Can't you just imagine God pointing out to Adam and Eve what had developed in the garden during the day—the fuzzy kiwi, the flaming crape myrtle?

Even when Eve chose self-trust over God-trust, Emmanuel still came close. Even when the pomegranate lay open and empty of its jewels, God killed an animal to sew clothes to protect them from the sun.

Later, after leading them through the Red Sea, He led the people of Israel by His presence through the desert with fire by night and cloud by day. And at first, He was visible but distant, in front of the people.

But that wasn't enough for Him. God longed for more.

He called Moses a friend and spoke to him face-to-face. His presence was with one person, but God wanted to *be with all* the people.

He had the Israelites build a tabernacle, a tent that could be taken down and moved. The ark of the covenant hid tangible symbols of His faithfulness—Aaron's rod that budded, manna—and now He was *beside* His people, next to the traveling caravans.

But that wasn't enough. Emmanuel longed for more.

He invited Solomon to build a temple, and when He came to reside within the thick-cut stone walls, He came heavy. And now *God* was present and accessible *inside* the city.

Yet Emmanuel still wanted more. God chose to take on a body, to place the pads of His feet on our streets, to get the dust of earth under His nails as *the* Emmanuel, the *God-with-us. And He positioned Himself to shepherd Israel as He searched for the hurting and the helpless from town to town.*

And when He died, that cross—His two arms out—became a bridge for Him to draw us close, a permanent way to the Father. When He died, the thick, chain mail curtain between us and the Holy of Holies tore. No barriers to the presence. He died so we could make our home in His presence.

Yet He *still* wanted more. He sent the Holy Spirit to reside *within* us.

And yet, He still wants more, to make us His bride. Revelation 21:2–3 (ESV) says, "And I saw the holy city, new Jerusalem, coming down out of heaven from God, prepared as a bride adorned for her husband. And I heard a loud voice from the throne saying, 'Behold, the dwelling place of God is with man. He will dwell with them, and they will be his people.'"

We have been brainwashed by the pain and brokenness of the world to believe that God's love could not possibly be that kind, that tender, that compassionate, that persevering, that forgiving, that steadfast, that unconditional, or that absolutely delightful. You, my friend, hold a unique place in His heart. His passionate pursuit of you will never wane until He is holding you in His arms.

Access group questions and push play on videos at summerjoy gross.com/the-emmanuel-promise, which includes a Lectio Divina on Revelation 21 among other resources.

9

Saint Patrick Shows the Way

For six years, the young man we now know as Saint Patrick woke up on the hills around Slemish Mountain, a cowherd and a kidnapped slave. When he was sixteen he was captured by raiders from a small Roman outpost in Britton, probably on the western coast of Wales. When he was sold to the chieftain Milchu in what is now County Antrim, it was the fifth century and a time of incredible danger. Clan against clan. Chief against chief. Druid against druid.

Although Patrick had been born into a Christian family—his grandfather a priest and his father a deacon—he had never chosen to follow Christ himself. Everything changed as he walked those hills as a slave. His fifth century autobiography says this: "I was constantly humbled through hunger and nakedness."[1] The book also describes how, in the midst of homelessness and captivity, God became Patrick's companion and lifeline.[2]

Six years later, he escaped. It was no easy task pushing through starvation and searching for a boat back to Britton's shore. But when he was back with his family, he had a dream. The Irish people were sending him a message: "Walk among us again." After weeks of dreams, he decided to voluntarily go back to his captors, this time filled with compassion and a desire for them to have the hope he knew in Christ. He began studying for priesthood—no short task. It took at least a decade, maybe two. He studied in Gaul at the monastery of Martin of Tours, learning Scripture and Latin, always the oldest in the room. Finally, he was ordained.

Although we know very little from his life, we know that back in Ireland he purposefully sought out his captor, the chieftain Milchu, who then became one of the first Christians on the island. Patrick also became an antislavery activist, which we know because we still have a letter demanding the release of slaves.

We also have this prayer, Saint Patrick's breastplate. These words were the shield he armed himself with daily as he chose to stride into danger, carrying little more than his faith. These were the words he used to pray through fear:

> Christ with me,
> Christ before me,
> Christ behind me,
> Christ in me,
> Christ beneath me,
> Christ above me,
> Christ on my right,
> Christ on my left,
> Christ when I lie down,
> Christ when I sit down,
> Christ when I arise,
> Christ in the heart of every man who thinks of me,
> Christ in the mouth of everyone who speaks of me,
> Christ in every eye that sees me,
> Christ in every ear that hears me.

Every morning, he visualized himself wrapped in the Emmanuel presence of God. With every phrase, he painted a picture of the day surrounded by Christ. Saint Patrick *lived* the promise that his core identity, as well as the foundation of his greatest safety, was the truth that he was encircled by Christ's presence. Patrick grounded his nervous system in the truth of God's nearness before setting out into his day.

God's Omnipresence throughout Scripture

God set the table in the wilderness with sensory reminders of His presence, a cloud by day, a pillar of fire by night, and daily manna to feed the Israelite families. He was training them to depend on His presence for every step and eat out of His hand. He was training them to look around them for visual reminders of His nearness.

Moses refused to move unless the presence was going with him. In Exodus 33:14, the Lord promised him: "My Presence will go with you, and I will give you rest."

I love how Moses answered, "If Your Presence does not go with us . . . do not lead us up from here. For how then can it be known that Your people and I have found favor in Your sight, unless You go with us? How else will we be distinguished from all the other people on the face of the earth?" (Exod. 33:15–16 BSB). He knew that his core identity was characterized by the presence of Jesus. Living without the presence was not an option.

In Psalm 16, David subdued his fear by visualizing God with him: "I have set the LORD always before me. Because He is at my right hand, I will not be shaken" (v. 8 BSB).

It's the main thread running through Psalm 23: "Even though I walk through the valley of the shadow of death, I will fear no evil, for You are with me" (v. 4 BSB).

In Psalm 139:9–10, David was practicing holding on to the presence in every eventuality his imagination could whip up: "If I rise on the wings of the dawn, if I settle on the far side of the sea, even there your hand will guide me, your right hand will hold me fast."

On Instagram I invited others to place their own worst fears, their "even-ifs," inside the same brackets as David in Psalm 139.

You try it out:

Even if _____ (e.g., I got cancer, my child wouldn't speak to me, my salary didn't cover my bills, I lost my job), Your hand will guide me; Your right hand will hold me fast.

For years, fear kept me running. I was afraid of getting scorched by future "even-ifs." But I've learned that all those fears dissipate when we come awake to the truth of the living Christ, attentive, responsive, and engaged in the middle of every future story. What if, when we follow an overactive imagination down the path, we discover His embodied presence? How would that transform our fear? We can literally rehearse God's holding us in our "even-ifs." Breakthrough comes as we place our future fears on the altar of this line, because in the presence of the Emmanuel, fear loses its power.

Emotional Object Constancy with God

Numerous authors have gone before us in practicing the presence of our Emmanuel. Brother Lawrence taught that practicing the presence could change ordinary dishwashing into abiding with God. Missionary Frank Laubach found that the loneliness of a Filipino island was made into a cathedral of joy in God's presence. Author Leanne Payne encouraged people that the doorway to a mature faith and ministry was always through practicing the presence of God. She encouraged people to begin practicing the truth of God's presence by simply repeating the words, "Lord, I thank You that You are here."[3]

In his devotional *My Utmost for His Highest*, Oswald Chambers wrote this: "Notion your mind with the idea that God is there. If once the mind is noticed along that line, then, when you are in difficulties, it is as easy as breathing to remember—Why, my Father knows all about it! It is not an effort, it comes naturally when perplexities press."[4]

How do we begin to paint a picture of our future with Christ in it? We start small. Very small.

We start one sensory reminder of the presence of God at a time. Some people watch the flicker of a candle set in front of their sink as they do dishes. My friend Jennie draws a small ink cross on her wrist, a daily, temporary tattoo. Others wear a bracelet, a necklace, or a ring. Still others diffuse a single fragrance through their house, choosing to remember God's presence each time they catch the scent. I use a clinging cross as I walk or a small silver cross left in the pocket of my coats. I finger it during errands out. My mom remembers the presence as she hears the sound of water from a tabletop water fountain in an upstairs hallway.

Get creative. Ask God what sensory reminder you could take through your day. By using a sensory reminder of the presence of our Emmanuel, we're slowly establishing object constancy.

Here's what Dr. Henry Cloud says about emotional object constancy:

> Over time, the child gradually internalizes his mother's care. He begins storing up memories of being comforted by her. In a sense, the child takes his mother in and stores her inside his memory. This internalization gives him a greater and greater sense of security. He has a storehouse of loving memories upon which to draw in his mother's absence.
>
> As this relationship gets stronger and stronger, the child reaches another milestone: he achieves "emotional object constancy."[5]

This is our goal with God, emotional object constancy, but as you can see, it is not a quick process. Emotional object constancy is the embodied sense of security that God's love is our home base. It's the crescendo of Romans 8. After pointing to the gift of grace through the cross and the power of the Spirit to transform us, Paul wants us to experience a love that steadies us through every eventuality:

Who shall separate us from the love of Christ? Shall trouble or hardship or persecution or famine or nakedness or danger or sword? As it is written:

> "For your sake we face death all day long;
> we are considered as sheep to be slaughtered."

No, in all these things we are more than conquerors through him who loved us. For I am convinced that neither death nor life, neither angels nor demons, neither the present nor the future, nor any powers, neither height nor depth, nor anything else in all creation, will be able to separate us from the love of God that is in Christ Jesus our Lord. (vv. 35–39)

Paul says that mature Christian faith means that through every storm and story, our foundation is the unshakable love of God. Have you ever glanced over those words and wondered if Paul had become warm and fuzzy? This is a man who was beaten, imprisoned for his faith, and found himself living through the horror of a shipwreck. This is a man whose life was anything *but* cozy and comfortable. But even in the midst of extreme suffering, Paul tells us that it was God's loving presence that empowered him while he was in chains. He wanted the same for those who came after him:

> I pray that out of his glorious riches he may strengthen you with power through his Spirit in your inner being, so that *Christ may dwell in your hearts* through faith. And I pray that you, being *rooted and established in love*, may have power, together with all the Lord's holy people, *to grasp how wide and long and high and deep is the love of Christ, and to know this love that surpasses knowledge—that you may be filled to the measure of all the fullness of God*. (Eph. 3:16–19, emphasis added)

Paul knew God's presence was where security lies even as hurricanes blustered, scars marred his skin, and men stood guard over him under house arrest. And God's love was his only security as martyrdom loomed.

Emmanuel Incognito

Contrary to popular belief, Saint Patrick's life never resembled frolicking in clover. Having escaped a life of starvation and slavery, he chose to sail back to Ireland where he was still considered someone's property. And there, the place of his greatest wounding became the place of his greatest ministry.

He didn't ignore his anxiety, he prayed *through* it. He did the hard work of envisioning truth, planting a cross in the midst of his imagination.

He didn't obey the message of his trauma; he chose to visualize the One who was wielding a sword on his behalf, the One who has angels at His beck and call.

Every morning, Saint Patrick visualized himself encircled by the presence before he walked out of his cottage. He proclaimed the ground he walked on consecrated by the real presence of the Trinity.

And *then*, he moved forward.

Locked Doors Cannot Keep Him Locked Out

After the crucifixion, the disciples huddled behind a locked door. It's understandable. They had seen their Jesus die. They had heard about how He had been wrapped and placed in a locked tomb. But our Emmanuel is not hindered by locked doors. He pursues us, even when we're huddled in the grip of our circumstances.

When Jesus walked through that wall, how do you think the disciples felt? Overwhelmed? Awed? Yes, all that. They also no longer felt alone. They no longer felt powerless because the power that calmed storms had arrived in the middle of their fear. Love incarnate had burst into their suffocating story. The Emmanuel was in the room. "Peace be with you" was the answer to their every question.

Monday Morning Practical: Emmanuel Is Here

We're going to practice recognizing the truth of the presence of God in the midst of our worry.

Think of an experience of everyday life that brings you anxiety: An actual place. An actual person. Look around the room. Where are you standing? Imagine the touch of the place. The smell of the place. Where are you sitting? Now, invite the embodied presence of Christ into the room. Watch how He comes in. How does His presence change the room? Stay right there for a moment. Enjoy His company.

Now, linger with these words:

The God who holds all the universe in order . . . is here.

The God who spoke and out came the Milky Way . . . is here.

The God who creates and recreates and lovingly makes a mosaic of all our broken pieces . . . is here.

The God who had you in mind before the foundation of the world . . . is here.

The God who sees you and knows how the brokenness of the world bears down on your shoulders . . . is here.

The God who hears the toxic swirl inside your mind and treats you tenderly . . . is here.

The God who knows how many hairs are on your head, who catches your tears in His bottl . . . is here.

The God who sets a table before you . . . is here.

This God walks with you through every door, down every trail, into every unknown. He is present with you.

> Christ with you,
> Christ before you,
> Christ behind you,
> Christ in you,
> Christ beneath you,
> Christ above you,
> Christ on your right,
> Christ on your left,
> Christ when you lie down,
> Christ when you sit down,
> Christ when you arise.

You are not alone. He wraps you in His presence. You are held.

Visit summerjoygross.com/the-emmanuel-promise and push play on the three videos for this chapter as often as you'd like. I'll lead you through a Monday Morning Practical and a Lectio Divina on Ephesians 3:16–19 and an Ignatian Imaginative Prayer practice of Jesus's resurrection appearance walking through locked doors.

10

Holy in the Mundane

Cliff swallows were darting around our pontoon, dipping onto the wide emerald-green ribbon of the Chattahoochee River to sip up mayflies. When Andrew bought the pontoon eighteen years ago, I cringed. Would it see enough water to warrant the sticker shock of eight hundred dollars? When it appeared on our front lawn, it came in a hundred parts, including a fly-fishing stand for the front. We would put it to bed in the back of Andrew's black Subaru Baja and drive west, reassembling it on the bank of the Yellowstone River during our summer vacation, pre-kids. For four days we floated the river and searched for its legendary trout, stopping for breakfasts of eggs and bacon and camping on the banks of the islands on the way down.

Eighteen years later, having floated hundreds of river miles, we had our waders on again, Andrew occasionally sliding off the chair of the same pontoon to anchor us on a granite rock in the river, giving us enough time to fish the riffles where trout might be hiding. Andrew's a fantastic fishing guide, intelligent and skilled, the kind who enjoys watching their protégé catch the fish. I'm happy to oblige.

Despite Andrew still being jet-lagged from a trip to Kigali, Rwanda, we had captured the day. While he was gone, I had been home wrangling kids and their evening sports. My mother had flown in to provide backup. We were smack-dab in the middle of a crushing season, a potential move, relational conflict with someone dear to us, a daughter stretching toward the sun and simultaneously struggling, and a college decision for our oldest.

We needed to slow time to the current of the river and choose to think only about swallows, where to cast our line, and the joy of netting rainbow trout for each other. We had come to the river to find a sanctuary of time. As I watched the swallows, words from Psalm 84:3 came to mind: "Even the sparrow has found a home, and the swallow a nest for herself . . . a place near your altar, LORD Almighty."

My nervous system began to quiet as I focused on the trout's potential hiding places and the swallows circling the pontoon. Andrew and I have one rule on days like this: enjoy each other's company. No deep discussions. No arguments. Just savoring. We may have been weighed down in a season of heaviness, but on this day, during these eight hours, we guarded joy.

We were having an anniversary of sorts, though we wouldn't realize it until we saw the date on the calendar later that evening. Thirty years prior, on April 23, we had ambled along the country lane below Andrew's house for our first date, glancing sideways into each other's eyes. One side of the road was carpeted with white trillium. Two years later on that same date, Andrew surprised me as he slipped a ring on my finger, a gold replica of my great-grandmother's ring, evergreens engraved on either side of the stone. Today we were giving each other the extravagant gift of resting in each other's presence.

The swallows darted and swooped in arcs across our horizon point, evading my attempts to capture them with my camera. I decided to just sit and memorize their flight patterns, slowing my attention to the present moment where I softly whispered to God, "You are here."

All of creation sings God's praises, and when surrounded by the queenly white sycamore, the scraggly, grandfather heron, and the dip and swirl of swallows, we were able to join the river's slow song of worship.

Present Moment Awareness

During times of intense stress, we struggle to be relational and, instead, stay stuck in survival mode. Our minds swoop into the future, manufacturing a story of fear. During those seasons, expecting ourselves to be present to God is an exercise in futility and, ultimately, in shame. It's neuroscience. When we're in survival mode, we either fight to control the present moment or dissociate to establish safety. We aren't present in our own bodies. How could we be present to God?

The first pathway to the presence is grounding in our bodies and grounding in the present moment. All neuroscientists agree, relationship connection occurs best in the present moment.[1] If we are calculating the future or ruminating on the past, we are not present to those right in front of us. Bringing our awareness to the Emmanuel is no different. It requires an inner stillness that is extremely difficult to maintain in our fast-paced life. Isaiah 30:15 addresses this internal wrestle: "In repentance and rest is your salvation; in quietness and trust is your strength, but you would have none of it."

When our bodies are grounded in the present moment, we are quiet enough to become attentive to the uninterrupted symphony of praise that rises from every corner of creation. Our nervous system calms, and we become available to the mixture of joy and sorrow we're carrying. We become available to each other. We also become available to Another.

In her poem "Flickering Mind," poet Denise Levertov wrote,

> Lord, not you
> It is I who am absent . . .
> I stop
> to think about you, and my mind

119

at once
like a minnow darts away.[2]

As Andrew and I floated down the Chattahoochee River, I thought about how easy it is to become consumed with *ephemera*, the thousands of details that make up a human life. We miss how God is present, steady like a stream. We can't see it until we allow ourselves to stop, to rest our brains by immersion in the senses, breathing in the woody smell of the river, watching the light dance on riffles, catching the mayfly as she struggles to emerge.

The Latin for mayfly, Andrew tells me, is "Ephemeroptera." The Renaissance artist Albrecht Dürer included the mayfly in a woodcut of the Holy Family, a nod to the juxtaposition between the solidity of God and the brief nature of life.

As we floated downstream, our phones got occasional pings from the kids, and we'd answer, but for the most part, we'd bracketed this moment. We'd walked the pontoon down the cement launch, and we couldn't take it out until we floated these few miles. We chose to become unavailable. For five hours, we chose a different relationship with time.

After weeks of single parenting while Andrew was in Rwanda, I was so wound up that it took a few hours floating on the river before I began praying, a few hours of rocks and riffles until we hit the second section of the river, where, besides downed trees, the river was ironed out into a wide, green ribbon. Instead of being frustrated with how wound up I was, I allowed the ironing out to happen naturally, my breaths growing deeper and deeper.

Slowly, I was able to dip into prayer. *Lord, is there anything You desire to say? Is there a word You'd like to speak into the quiet?* I've discovered the beauty of holding an open-ended question with God, not demanding an answer but inviting connection.

What if we just enjoyed each other's company, receiving the gift of resting in each other's presence, of giving each other the gift of extravagantly wasting time together? As poet Walt Whitman is often paraphrased, "We were together. I forget the rest."[3] Relationship, even relationship with God, occurs in the present moment, but so often, we are distracted elsewhere. Our senses root us in the here and now. Present moment awareness is the on-ramp to practicing His presence.

A Practical On-Ramp to Presence during Life's Storms

Sometimes anxiety keeps us amped up and we're unable to notice the nourishment our Emmanuel is sending moment by moment. We are hurried and harried, surging from one agenda to another while life with Emmanuel passes us by. His invitation to "be still, and know that [He is] God" (Ps. 46:10) is nearly impossible in the midst of heightened suffering, whether it's financial worries, relational pain, or a possible diagnosis that's still being tested at the lab. Even amid the pain, God spreads a table for us in the wilderness, providing for us in our suffering.[4] Surprisingly, gratitude that grows naturally from present moment awareness can become the way we scoot up to His table.

Andrew and I had been serving shoulder to shoulder with our church in South Haven, Michigan, for nine years when an argument threatened to scatter our parish. Two families sat on opposite sides of the aisle.

They were (and are) beautiful people. Stunning. It was a privilege to minister with them, a privilege to place the Eucharist inside their empty palms, a privilege to throw burgers on the grill and play cornhole in the summer, a privilege to do kingdom work side by side.

But you know the story. An argument became a lightning rod for fear or frustration, and then all of a sudden, people who had prayed and cried together, fought and stood together, were no longer talking. Or worse yet, they *were* talking, just not to us. It could have started a hundred different ways, but a small, contained fire became raging anger with a bit of the gasoline of self-righteousness. And we all had our share of that. On Sunday mornings they made excuses to stay home. Or go to the lake. Or go north to their cabin. Our numbers dwindled while our anxiety shot up.

That summer we were afraid our small outpost of the kingdom was going to be knocked over like dominoes. Those two months I woke with my jaw tight with anxiety. I ate anxiety with my Mini-Wheats. I walked down the sidewalks toward the farmer's market gripping anxiety tighter than the bags I brought home.

Stilling my mind was as difficult as stopping the merry-go-round at the local park while the kids were twirling. I tried practicing gratitude, writing down gifts as Ann Voskamp taught in *One Thousand Gifts*. But here's the thing. My anxiety was so debilitating that I needed an on-ramp to gratitude. Anxiety had me caught by the ankles. I was held tight by fear.

But I *could* sit down and run my fingers through the grass. I could sit down and open my ears to the creaking of the swing as it went back and forth as my little girl pumped her legs. I could lie back and watch one small cloud puff make its way across the sky.

I could lie back onto the earth, taking my place in it. I am dust and to dust I will return, and sometimes the stuff of earth as we turn it over in our hands, smelling the damp soil, becomes a doorway to presence. The on-ramp to noticing Emmanuel's presence turned out to be something I could literally taste and touch, a grounding in the senses.

Let's make this Monday morning practical. Ten Minutes of Stillness is a ten-minute soul vacation. The more we do this, the more our brains practice setting down rumination and settling into the goodness of the present moment. Want to learn how to hold suffering and joy at the same time? This beautiful practice, tweaked from Dr. Daniel Siegel's book *Aware*, is one of the keys.

First, focus on one sense at a time. For that one minute, your only job is to experience that sense. Open up to the sound of the cars rushing past, the hum of the refrigerator, the birdsong outside your window. The only rule—no judging or meaning-making. Purely focus on receiving the sensory information available to you. After cycling through each sense, spend one full minute opening your awareness to all five senses at once. Next, name the simple things that are bringing you joy. What are you thankful for that you are presently experiencing? Tell Jesus. Name the points of joy around you. Finally, just rest with Jesus, enjoying the present moment together.[5]

Remember, stilling your mind in the present moment is a necessity for relationship and ultimately, for practicing the presence of our Emmanuel.

When I moved into gratitude, I staggered into a feast. What I was not expecting was that this on-ramp would deepen my ability to experience the present moment. I was Dorothy in the *Wizard of Oz*, going from black and white to technicolor. Neuroscientist Daniel Siegel describes it this way: "Mental presence is a state of being wide awake and receptive to what is happening, as it is happening in the moment, within us and between the world and us. Presence cultivates happiness."[6]

Put even more simply, we won't experience God's presence if we are not present ourselves. When our brains are wound up, shooting

Monday Morning Practical: Ten Minutes of Stillness

1. Hearing—What do you hear? Street noise? Wind through the trees? Listen without filtering.
2. Vision—What do you see? Let your eyes focus on one square foot.
3. Touch—What do you feel? Feel your feet on the ground, your body on the bench, the wind on your skin.
4. Smell—What do you smell? What does the air smell like?
5. Taste—What do you taste? Are you having a cup of coffee? Take a sip. Focus on the milky bitterness.
6. All five—For one minute, open all five senses at once.
7–8. Gratitude—What are you experiencing through your senses that you are thankful for? Tell Jesus.
9–10. Practicing His presence—Just enjoy His company. He's experiencing what you're experiencing.

into an unknown future or still stuck rehearsing yesterday's whys, we are still in fight-or-flight mode. We only sit before the I AM with our shoes off in the burning bush of the present moment.

Practicing the present moment and getting grounded in the here and now are the on-ramp for the Emmanuel promise, living moment by moment *with* God. The senses ground us. They teach us to settle right here. They teach our bodies that we are safe. We stop fighting for safety, and our anxious spirituality is carefully wrapped and soothed.

When we're grounded and centered, we have ample internal space to turn toward our Emmanuel and receive His attentive presence. Remember how you feel when someone you love comes to you with spontaneous gratitude? Your heart swings wide open toward them. In fact, neuro-theologian and author Jim Wilder tells us that gratitude is right next to our relational brain.[7] Gratitude opens the door to deeper relationship.

In Psalm 131:2, David uses the imagery of a baby, peaceful and quiet after they cease nursing: "I have stilled and quieted my soul; like a weaned child with its mother, like a weaned child is my soul within me" (BSB). We used to call the moments after our babies finished nursing *milk drunk*, when they looked pleased and full and loved. There's a similarity to when we've sunk down into the blessing of our present moment. We sing our hallelujahs. When we sink right down into our senses, tasting the present, we are surprised that there's joy enough right here. We no longer have to fight for it. We no longer have to strain for it.

As poet Derek Walcott wrote, "Sit. Feast on your life."[8]

As we become awake to the present, we discover a doorway to attentiveness. And once again, as we become open and available, Emmanuel is ready to burst through the veneer between us.

This Is Where the Healing Begins

By now I'm sure you're wondering what happened to the precious group of people, bound together in a church. What occurred was a miracle of the humblest kind. One day the simple words "I love you" became the emergency paddles of an electrical shock and life rushed right back in.

We witnessed resurrection.

And, friends, I wish you could have been there the following Sunday to see the welcome. The hugs. The whispers of "Peace be with you" and "And also with you" spoken while looking into each other's eyes, tears streaming. Corporate repentance. True, beautiful humility. Then we resealed our communion as we shared the common cup.

I could have held my breath that whole time. I could have lost an entire summer. But at night I would sit on the back porch with a hot tea in my hand, a cool breeze playing around my shoulders, and my head back searching for a shooting star. And whether I saw one or not, the truth is that I was present. I sat down on the canvas of a captain's chair, and my anxiety was forgotten for at least ten minutes. And the next day? Twenty. And the next? A few glorious hours of freedom.

In this next section, we are going to get even more practical. I find it unkind when people stay comfortably shrouded in esoteric theology. We are left holding a vague destination but not knowing how to get there. We can feel overwhelmed and abandoned, and shame can take root easily. I don't want to do that to you.

These are the Christian practices—most ancient, some new—that have been essential in my journey to secure attachment. They have also been essential for the hundreds of others I've had the privilege to walk with over the last fourteen-plus years. The Holy Spirit, your ardent Companion, will lead you to others. As always, ask God for a community to travel with. Journeying together will be an essential part of your healing.[9]

Let's go deeper! Pour yourself a cuppa and access videos of Psalm 131:2, the Ten Minutes of Stillness, and other grounding exercises at summerjoygross.com/the-emmanuel-promise.

PART II

INTRODUCTION TO ATTACHMENT PRACTICES

God is always looking for doorways in. He knocks, His ear against the grain of the wood, leaning forward in expectation, hand on the doorknob, waiting for when we are undistracted enough to come awake to His presence. He's waiting for an invitation. He's waiting for us to become open, available . . . hungry. The attachment practices I've included in this section are some of the most powerful doorways I've found.

When I first discovered how much my attachment style was affecting my adult relationships, carving a sin pattern through my brain, I stumbled around in grief. It's natural to lament what could have been, but please don't let discouragement derail the work of healing the Emmanuel is inviting you into. It's time to allow the awareness of your attachment wound to propel you into action, allowing the Spirit to transform you from insecure to secure.

It's time to get Monday morning practical.

The next nine chapters are invitations to practical pathways for attachment with God.

There are countless helpful books on spiritual disciplines. In compiling this list, I was not seeking to be thorough, but to provide you with a list of practices that will nourish your journey. Guided by the Holy Spirit, you will discover other disciplines. Remember, God is initiating. We are responding.

I remember the concept of "abiding with God" being preached from the pulpit when I was young and folding inward in shame. I saw the way a woman at my church clung to Jesus as she walked through breast cancer, but for me, abiding felt like an impossibility. Discouraged by my tendency to be "prone to wander," I saw the invitation to abide with God as one more way I wasn't able to measure up.

Here are some things it would have been helpful to know:

1. Building a secure attachment with God is not a quick process. It's Spirit-led, not formulaic. The renewing of the mind takes time.

2. The Spirit will empower you for the journey. Give Him responsibility. Fall into His waiting arms over and over again. And when you stumble, Saint Benedict invites you "always" to "begin again."

3. You were never meant to do this on your own. As you find others on the journey, you will discover a jet stream. Their faith will propel your faith.

4. When you try something new, it can feel clunky and awkward. Don't give up. If you don't have a group to do this with, find a spiritual director to lead you.

5. Be curious about what makes you uncomfortable. What's arising within you? Is there a story there? Does God want you to press into your discomfort?

6. Don't skimp on quieting/grounding. If your mind is still buzzing, you won't be able to receive. Remember, God is always present. Your main task is to be present with Him.

7. Read about each of the practices in the section below and then ask the Spirit which one is for you. Start there.

8. Keep a journal. This can include letters and laments and listening. We are a forgetful people, virtual sieves. You'll want to take notes so the Spirit can remind you of places He's met you before.

Again, the practices listed in this book are not the only practices God will use to draw you close. You are on an adventure, and the invitation of the Spirit will encourage you to explore spiritual disciplines that may surprise you. He may give you a desire to engage a new practice or He may kindly lead you to a place that stretches you where you will eventually experience a "spacious place."

There are many practices I didn't include. Sometimes they didn't make it in because of the available space between these two covers; sometimes I left them out because others have written about them with such thoughtfulness. Music is one of the practices I hoped to include. I believe the current trend of singing long sets of praise music is actually people working out their attachment with God in an embodied way. Our right-brain emotional centers are accessed through music. We borrow the language of lament, and tears are allowed to flow. We open our palms to receive the lullaby of the Father. We surrender and move toward trust, and we soak in love. Just as importantly, we receive new and life-altering vistas of the character of God. When we worship *with* the body of Christ, we remember all the resources sitting in the pews around us.

There's much brain science around singing and music about how our brains are integrated and our nervous systems are calmed. The 2023 Asbury College revival gave us a peek at the healing power of God's love as people stayed in the presence of God while the students played worship music. In the past, enslaved African Americans made it through centuries of horror by singing laments and receiving God's nearness through hours of corporate worship. I also love how this practice usually occurs in community. Again, when we do life together, we position ourselves in the jet stream of growth.

Practices involving joy and gratitude have been written about by others, but they are absolutely essential for building an attachment with God.[1] Why? Our brains naturally slide to the negative, creating a protective layer to guide us away from harm. It is said that the negative is Velcro, and the positive is Teflon. The problem is God's provision is easily forgotten, and our memories become skewed. It takes conscious repetition of the abundant gifts of God to build trust.[2] Purposeful gratitude and recalling sensory-filled moments[3] renews our minds so we start to believe our Father truly *does* give His children good gifts.[4] We remember the table He sets in the wilderness, and we are healed in the remembering.

The list of practices is endless. Sabbath. Retreating. Worship. Study. Taking communion. The important thing is to follow the movement of the Holy Spirit and walk with a group who is also finding their way to attachment and resting in the heart of God. Again, if you'd like to join a small group or monthly retreat with the Presence Project, we'd love to have you.

What's important to remember is that these practices are not exams to pass or works to prove your worthiness. These are invitations from your Emmanuel. This is how you tune your ears to His persistent knock, turn the knob, and open the door to fall into His waiting arms.

11

A Tangible Reminder

Building Awareness

Definition: As we light a candle, finger a cross in our pocket or on a piece of jewelry, or engage in any other of a number of tangible reminders, we are building awareness that our Emmanuel is present.

Attachment Principle: In training our minds to be aware of God's nearness, we develop the first step of attachment, object constancy. Why? In order to build attachment with our new adoptive Father, we must first believe that He is present and available.

Scripture: "I WILL NEVER [under any circumstances] DESERT YOU [nor give you up nor leave you without support, nor will I in any degree leave you helpless], NOR WILL I FORSAKE *or* LET YOU DOWN *or* RELAX MY HOLD ON YOU [assuredly not]!" (Heb. 13:5 AMP).

The eastern branch of the Huron River ran through my family's property when I was growing up. It wasn't much more than a creek, but it was our creek. Crawdads skittered under rocks, and the water flowed cold, even in August.

We had bought the house from a contractor who built the house as a love letter for his wife who was struggling with breast cancer.

Every room was embellished with thoughtfulness. Between the family room and the kitchen, he installed swinging doors with stained glass from an area hospital that was being renovated. He collected bricks from a kiln in southern Ohio, rebuilding it on the hill. Oddly enough, he also disposed of a pile of flat cement blocks in the creek. Perhaps he was trying to dam it up. Perhaps it was creative inspiration that was then too heavy to correct. But those flat cement blocks in the creek became my favorite place to unwind after school. As the water flowed, something loosened in my brain. The cement blocks made for a poor illustration of a waterfall, but they were my waterfall. And in the confusion of junior high, that became my favorite place to pray.

A few years ago, in February, Andrew and I bundled up the kids and drove into the North Georgia mountains for a hike along Hemlock Falls. It was my idea of the perfect hike—a slow ascent, umbrella-shaped rhododendron arching over the trail, and a river skipping down the mountain on one side.

Halfway through the hike, I slipped my hand into the pocket of my anorak and discovered the clinging cross I had left there the year before. It's called a clinging cross because it's ergonomically designed with grooves for our fingers to grasp. We are an embodied people, and when we engage our bodies in prayer, we often discover new doorways to conversation with God.

Through high school, I'd pass my mom's study early in the morning on the way to the bathroom before school and see her kneeling at the blue couch, Bible open. Now in our Anglican church, I too settle my knees into a cushioned kneeler, preparing my heart for confession. Our posture can position us to engage the holy with our full attention. Our *bodies*, not just our souls, were meant for prayer.

Grasping a tiny wooden cross as I take a walk has become a way for me to stay attentive to the presence of God. As I grasp the cross, I'm reminded that He and I are attentive to the same present moment, the same present experience. I can jump from present moment awareness to prayer through the single act of clinging. Hiking the North Georgia mountains on that warm February day, I was grasping for a quiet heart and mind.

The Prayerful Practice of Paying Attention

I am a product of a people addicted to technology and its false promises of productivity. During busy seasons with constant streams of text messages and notifications, I practice the presence of my smartphone. Sometimes I sit at Starbucks working and recognize I'm not the only one.

We are all practicing the presence of something.

As I squeezed the hard resin of the clinging cross that February day, I remembered a simple prayer question, a way to become alert and listen for God's voice: *Jesus, what is it You wish to say to me through this experience right now?*

Theologian and author Richard Foster says that paying attention is the greatest need of this generation, and if he were to rewrite his spiritual classic *Celebration of Discipline*, he would have included attentiveness as a necessary spiritual discipline.[1] Prayer has become an even greater struggle in a world of beeps and buzzes and easily attainable information. Sometimes staying present to the voice of God takes an intentional grasping, a clinging.

There are umpteen things you can use as a reminder of the presence of God, but here's what I love about the clinging cross. Jesus didn't just die for sins on that cross, He elected to carry all the suffering and pain of the world. When we grasp the cross, we remember that we are not carrying our pain alone.

At the end of a Kenyan Eucharistic liturgy and before the blessing, participants are invited to turn toward the cross and say these words, making a large gesture toward the cross with each phrase:

> All our problems,
> We send to the cross of Christ!

All our difficulties,
We send to the cross of Christ!
All the devil's works,
We send to the cross of Christ!
All our hopes,
We set on the risen Christ![2]

As we grasp the cross, we practice giving Christ what's impossible for us to bear. We set our hope on the power of the risen Christ.

A Spiritual Autobiography in Waterfalls

During the hike, I kept fingering the clinging cross and asking that question: "Jesus, what is it You wish to say?" I waited. Sometimes as I wait for an answer from God, I don't hear anything. I don't force connection through words. I experience the silence as an invitation to companionship. That particular day, as I waited, my mind focused on the sound of the river tossing over the rocks. As I continued hiking, I began remembering waterfalls of my life. Ever since that makeshift waterfall in the creek in our side yard, I've sought them out. By now, there's half a lifetime of waterfalls, and that February day, those waterfalls suddenly seemed as intentional as an arc along a storyline.

But my mind was honing in on one particular waterfall. Just out of college, when Andrew and I traveled to L'Abri, Switzerland, we hiked to a handful of waterfalls, one of which was down a path between Huemoz and Villars. This waterfall was ferociously loud, a torrent. That spring I yelled, I wept, and I worshiped in a furious unloading of pain.

Back in Georgia, as I thought of the waterfall in Switzerland, I fingered the cross and tried to grasp the Word starting to bubble up within me. I held tight to the question, What is it You wish to say? For a moment I just walked silently, waiting. I thought of Switzerland and the original confusion of a woman unsure she could trust God's goodness. I remembered the original tangle of lies and the constant companion of shame. And just for a moment, in my imagination, the risen Christ sat down next to me on that rock. Just His presence shifted the memory. Because if I've learned anything as a healing prayer minister, I've learned that when the Light of the World walks into pain, He scatters the darkness. I could feel tears rising to the surface. "Summer, do you see how your suffering has been redeemed?" He asked. "Your wounds have become the path through which you minister. Nothing has been lost. Do you hear Me? Nothing has been wasted."

In that instant, still grasping on to the cross, all of my brokenness shifted over into meaning. There was an arc to my story. Although my pain had been caused by the consequences of human brokenness, God had not allowed it to swallow me. He had not allowed it to be the end of the story. My greatest pain had become the source of God's flow of ministry through me.

I grasped the cross and tears fell hot, tears that tasted of gratefulness. A long-awaited release. I had finally moved from the cross to resurrection. And nothing had been wasted.

Let's continue making this practical together. You can access videos with reflection questions and a Lectio Divina on Lamentations 3:22–23 to encourage you to walk with God through the ordinary moments of your day at summerjoygross.com/the-emmanuel-promise.

12

Posture

Embodied Expectation

Definition: By using a simple posture, we can practice the presence of God through both joy-filled and emotionally heavy days.

Attachment Principle: We feel abandoned easily. It's easy to forget that Emmanuel has promised His presence. A prayer posture is a simple way to stay attentive to the One who is always attentive to us.

Scripture: "Pray without ceasing" (1 Thess. 5:17 ESV).

Try a Prayer Posture

Our body posture often influences our heart posture. We kneel in humility. We lay face down as we cry out to God in grief. Experiment. Just extending your arms in a cruciform posture of vulnerability can bring you into a more openhearted posture before God. Here are some other options.

- Turning your ear upward as if you are listening
- Keeping your palm open as a way of staying attentive

- Placing a hand over our heart so you can stay present to both your heart and God's compassion simultaneously
- Occasionally stretching out your hands in worship and/or as a child reaching out to their caregiver
- Crossing yourself often throughout the day—this can express many things
- Bowing your head in prayerful humility
- Lifting your face to God as if to a warm sun as Jesus did before feeding the five thousand

Get curious. What body posture could help you stay prayerfully in the presence of God as you move about your day?

Praying through the Busyness

I prayed, *"Come, Lord Jesus. Come"* into the frantic busyness of my morning.

I had only just found out family would start to arrive at noon for Caedmon's graduation. There was no time for an extended prayer time, but that didn't mean my soul didn't need it.

I needed to pray as I checked things off my list. *Is there a posture I can take to stay aware of the presence of God?* I wondered. I determined to turn my palm upwards in a posture of prayer as I moved around the kitchen from square to square of white tiles. Prayer postures are invitations to stay present to deep inner work as our bodies remind our hearts to pray.

The upwards palm reminds me of Sunday mornings at the altar rail, waiting shoulder to shoulder for the bread and wine. As I kneel on the cushions, I raise one hand over the other like a beggar asking for bread. As I turn my palm up, I admit my neediness. I admit my need for Emmanuel's presence.

It was not yet eight in the morning, and I'd already been running at full speed. I took Maddie to school, scurried through the grocery store grabbing items for the weekend, folded the laundry on the couch, and started roasting chicken for the noon meal. A stack of dishes sat in the sink begging for my attention. Steam rose from the boiling water on the stove, ready for the pasta. I poured the box of rotini in and then turned my palm back up.

Even though I knew my Emmanuel was present, with my palm raised, I kept my attention on my Divine Caregiver, staying attached, inviting Him into one of the tenderest moments of motherhood, the letting go. "I can't do this alone," I whispered. My oldest son was graduating the next day. "He may be leaving home soon, but You've got him, right? You'll continue to hold him in the palm of Your hand ten hours away at college?"

My youngest, Xavier, bounded down the stairs and slid onto a barstool at the kitchen island. It was his last day of seventh grade. I added French toast and morning conversation to the already packed itinerary.

It was Xavier's birth, fourteen years earlier, that sent me searching through my upstairs library for the slim book *Practicing the Presence of God* by Brother Lawrence. I could sense a tsunami of overwhelm headed my direction. How do you have time to pray when you have three children under five running about the place, kicking soccer balls off the baseboards of the dining room, and stripping clothes in favor of superhero costumes on Sunday morning before church? My need for the nearness of God did not lessen in the flurry of demands. If anything, my needs skyrocketed. My time was spoken for by these tiny souls. As I began to read Brother Lawrence's book, I was asking, How can I stay near my Emmanuel during the onslaught of the upcoming season?

Brother Lawrence would understand. His was not a quiet existence. For fifteen years, Brother Lawrence was principal cook in the monastery kitchen, feeding over a hundred men three times a day and overseeing every aspect of food preparation, even taking a barge downriver to collect provisions. He was essentially running a restaurant. In Paris, no less. He did all of this while in pain, limping from a war injury and struggling with complex PTSD. Beaufort, a young Parisian priest and eventually his biographer, said Brother Lawrence "often relived in his mind the dangers of his days in military service."[1] Brother Lawrence wrote that these memories caused him "horror."

Beaufort says this in *The Profile of Brother Lawrence*,

> Brother Lawrence began by frequently cultivating in his heart this exalted awareness of God's presence, contemplated by faith. By continual acts of adoration, love, and requests for our Friend's help in what he had to do, he sustained this conversation. Then, after completing a task, he thanked God.... Instead of diverting him from his work, his prayers helped him do it well.[2]

Brother Lawrence did small things with "great love."[3] Back in my kitchen, I continued to hold my palm up as I bustled around, squeezing lemons into the food processor, and toasting pinenuts in the frying pan. The olive oil around the chicken breast crackled as it roasted. At six thirty the next morning, we'd pile into cars and watch over seven hundred kids walk across a platform. They'd be handed a green folder with their diploma tucked inside. I already anticipated the grief of separation that welled up in my body every time I heard "Pomp and Circumstance." I was fully aware I needed the presence of Jesus like a lifeline. I held my palm up, listening, moving deliberately around the kitchen. *Jesus, be near*, I prayed.

This prayer posture was a continual conversation that spanned the practical to the personal. Just with this one posture, I was engaging God in a running conversation:

- Jesus, do you have anything You want to say?
- I want to follow Your lead.
- Come into this busy moment, Abba. I want You to be in charge.

- What should I do next?
- More manna, please.
- You're here, right? Please remind me You are near.

Everywhere I turned in the house, something was undone. Beds were unmade. Flowers plunked into pots after their arrival from the garden store were still waiting to be planted. The desk had last week's mail strewn across the surface. If I panicked, I would have little of myself to offer. I've learned that I have a choice: a panicked version of strained perfection or presence.

What Could Following Jesus Look Like as His Beloved?

A few years back, I was in training to become a spiritual director. I was emotionally wrung out after practicing holding the heavy stories of my fellow students and pulling up pieces of my own spiritual journey.

The flicker of the candles placed around the floor bounced off the dark windows of the common room. It was early evening, but because it was December, it was already dark. A large canvas labyrinth made up of black lines and circles, almost like a maze, was rolled out onto the Berber carpet. White pillar candles in glass jars were posted around. The room was hushed.

There's nothing magical about a labyrinth. It might look like a maze, but its lines and circles are just a simple way for people to pray while walking slowly, an embodied metaphor for walking with God. We stayed present as our socks hit the canvas. We nailed our attention down as we stepped forward. Heel, toe. Heel, toe. As our bodies joined our spirits, we became attentive. For millennia, Christians have been engaging their bodies in prayer. Kneeling. Holding out hands. Crying out face down. The labyrinth is just one more way to stay present to God in a culture of waning focus.

Maybe you've heard about people who took a year off to think and walk the Appalachian Trail before making a major job change.

They held a question as they walked it out, one mountain at a time. Transition requires attendance.

During the medieval time period, people believed spiritual transformation and going on pilgrimage were tied together. If we strip some of the unhelpful trappings off this concept, we're left with people who understood spiritual growth was a journey. They believed what happened to their internal lives was impacted by their bodies. The first labyrinth was created in the floor of Chartres Cathedral as a way to help people "walk out their prayer" if pilgrimage and leaving home was not an option.

I grew up in a tradition that believes there's a tie between intercession and prayer walking. It felt natural. I also grew up in a world that was tied to the values of striving and busyness. As a product of my culture, I needed a way to still my mind, to quiet myself, to be focused in prayer. Walking with God is one of the ways I've learned to stay attentive to the One who is always attentive to me.

In fact, whenever God is inviting me to make a shift in my spiritual life, I have a desire to go on pilgrimage, to strip distractions, to stay present to His invitation, step-by-step. To talk it out with God. To walk it out.

Michelle, our leader as we walked the labyrinth that December night, invited us to wrestle with this question, "Is there a prayer posture you can take to stay aware of the presence of God?" As I waited for my turn on the labyrinth, my mind went back to a memory.

It was a Healing Care Group from several years ago. The theme of that evening's teaching was trust, and we were invited to do a trust walk. I was blindfolded, and Marie Diebold, another member, led me through her own farmhouse kitchen. She knew every step, every obstacle—like the small stairstep from the dining room to the kitchen. She walked it backwards, holding on to my hands. I felt safe without sight, knowing who I was following, her face turned toward me.

That December night, as I stepped onto the canvas labyrinth, I sensed Jesus's invitation to practice walking in prayer as though

I was holding His hands through the trust exercise. In my mind, Jesus was walking backwards as Marie Diebold had, face attentive toward me.

I walked, palms up, imagining His hands holding mine. I would take a few steps and then sense the Lord inviting me to stop and rest, to take a deep breath, to pray and wait until I was fueled with energy again. In a labyrinth, we aren't being rushed toward a finish line. Our pace is our pace. Presence is the goal. As I continued forward, I sensed Jesus, patient and tender with my humanness.

A Prayerful Pace

As part of a generation striving toward an unattainable goal of perfection, I've always felt this verse was kind.

> As a father has compassion on his children,
>> so the LORD has compassion on those who fear him;
> for he knows how we are formed,
>> he remembers that we are dust. (Ps. 103:13–14)

Since God remembers our frailty, He knows our pace needs to be human. He's not a severe coach on the sidelines of our life demanding faster strides.

I always imagined following Jesus looked like trying to catch glimpses of a robe moving in and out of sight fifty yards down the path. I imagined sliding over rocks going downhill, having to yell to get His attention if I fell. I imagined surprise detours and a game of hide-and-seek. I imagined getting lost and struggling to find my way back. Alone.

Yet, if we are His children, adopted and beloved, He knows how He created us and the pace at which we can follow Him. What if following Jesus doesn't mean we have to force our feet to move faster, to run a race? What if following Jesus is a companioning at a human pace, practicing His presence? What if we can be *more* present to those around us, kingdom-minded, if we are spacious people, open-palmed people? It's hard to delight in anyone else when we're pinched, tightfisted, and striving. Walking the labyrinth in the dusk of that evening at the residency transformed my view of following Jesus. It informed my pace the morning of Caedmon's graduation and helped me stay present with my Emmanuel, palm open, even as my feet busily moved over the ordinary white tile of my kitchen.

We are God's beloved children, and He doesn't push us away, running off, demanding we keep up. He invites us to follow as He holds our hands, step by step.

———

Find a Lectio Divina video of Psalm 103:13–14 and other resources that go along with this chapter at summerjoygross.com /the-emmanuel-promise. All you have to do is push play. I'll lead you through.

13

Repentance

Turning toward the Father

Definition: In repentance, we ask for the forgiveness of the Father for a specific sin, desiring to come back in alignment with His kingdom purposes for us, His beloved children.

Attachment Principle: Receiving grace is difficult for those with attachment wounds. When we sin, either we feel like we've done something irreparable to our bond and stay bound in grief or we don't confront our sin at all in self-reliant avoidance. Because of our refusal, we don't experience the freedom and healing that come with repentance. Our Abba Father has not turned away. It's His kindness that leads us to repentance. Love does not leave us bound.

Scripture: "God's kindness leads us to repentance" (Rom. 2:4 BSB). "The Lord is not slow in keeping his promise, as some understand slowness. Instead he is patient with you, not wanting anyone to perish, but everyone to come to repentance" (2 Pet. 3:9).

How to Repent

Recognize: Ask for help. We don't even repent without the Spirit's help. Name specific choices and actions that the

Holy Spirit has identified as sinful. Speak out before the Lord that all these actions have cost. What has this sin cost spiritually, physically, emotionally, relationally? Ask God to give you an image of the cost.

Repent: Turn away from sin and turn toward God for help and healing. Agree that sin is not part of His plan and admit that what God has identified as sin is clearly sin.

Renounce: Renounce any involvement the evil one may have in this problem, bringing yourself thoroughly under the blood-bought victory of Jesus Christ.

Receive: Write down your acceptance of the forgiveness and cleansing that is yours in Jesus Christ. Voice the benefits of grace as a dearly loved child. Ask God to fill all that is lacking in you with the resurrection power of the Holy Spirit.

Realign: Seek the Lord's help in making specific changes in your lifestyle related to the sin you are confessing. Pray, *Lord, what changes would You encourage me to make?*

Rejoice: Give thanks for God's cleansing work. Refocus your attention on His character and power to "raise us from the dead."

Rest: Come home and rest in the presence of God as a dearly loved child, cleansed, accepted, delighted in. Give God permission to lead you in restoration and leave it in His hands.[1]

I wonder if Jesus helped unwrap Lazarus. Did He rush in and pull at the grave clothes, freeing His friend from death's grip? Did Jesus laugh as Lazarus untwisted, stretching out his arms, pulling at the cloth holding them down? Or did Jesus crouch in joy watching Lazarus, eyes blinking from the sun as he looked toward each sister with love and then gazed at his friend with astonishment?

Repentance is God's invitation to be unbound, to live in the light unhindered. It is part of God's greatest delight, His joy-filled rescue mission.

Dear friends, I wonder how it breaks the heart of God to see us bound. Christ's salvation work on the cross has raised us from the dead, but we're still wrapped tight in behaviors that keep us from walking free. When we are bound tight, we still have one foot in the grave, experiencing more hell than heaven. With a call to repentance, the Lord invites us to "Come out!" of the grave, to be released from death's grip.

We sit in the dark and cold of the tomb, no longer its resident but still not completely free. And if we can't experience His abundant life, it only ekes out of us, mixed with the bile still emerging from unprocessed pain. We stand before Him, far from the image of creative life He had in mind when He made us. I imagine Him with kindness, yelling out, "Unbind him. Unbind her. Let my child go."

Love, my friends, will not leave us bound.

He does not turn away, leaving us abandoned, expecting us to "deal" with our own sin, to clean ourselves up, to make ourselves presentable. We are covered by the full power of the cross. God *always* moves toward. We don't have to fear His presence moving away in disgust.

My Story of Discipline

When I was seventeen years old, I was driving the family minivan home late one night after theater rehearsal. After hitting a patch of black ice on Route 61, just three miles from home, the van spun and jolted, rolling up an embankment. I landed upside down in a farmer's side yard. He must have called the police right away because I was still hanging from the seat belt when multiple flashlights shined inside the window. I was cut free and inched my way out of the half-crushed frame. The police officer knew my dad, a local surgeon who worked with law enforcement as a county coroner when needed. That felt like grace. I was disoriented but known. He called my father and assured him I was okay, and Dad rushed over. He's wonderful in crisis. Always asking the right questions. Compassionate and concerned.

A year later, I was driving Dad's boxy, black Oldsmobile sedan, tired and distracted on my way home from school. I was turning left close to the drive-in theater when I rear-ended the car in front of me. Even if they had slammed on their brakes, it was still my fault. I was given a court date.

Staring out the long windows in the hallway just off the court-room, Dad and I looked outside at cars going past. He was tired. He may have even given me a "talking to" as we stood there staring out the window. I probably would do the same with my kids. The judge was lenient, requiring only a fine, but I felt like I had let my dad down, as if he would never again look at me with respect. Maybe he was just concerned, thinking about the family's upcoming move to Philadelphia, where he was taking considerable risk to leave a strong surgical practice and pursue a new degree in pediatric surgery. I chose to stay in Ohio that June, nannying for a family friend while I waited for college to begin in the fall. I shared a Jack and Jill bathroom with a sweet two-year-old named Abby who would climb onto my bed like a puppy early in the morning, looking at me until I opened my eyes.

In any case, because the move came so close on the heels of that court date, I never experienced a strong sense of repair. I went to college feeling like a disappointment. I wouldn't see Dad again until Thanksgiving, and for years, I struggled to feel close to him again. When the family drove away on their way to Philadelphia, I was left holding lies about his feelings toward me. "You are ditzy." "You are irresponsible." "You are a disappointment." I'm quite sure he didn't say any of those words, but for me, *discipline* was wired with *disappointment* and, finally, with *abandonment*.

Your Story of Discipline

Our early stories of discipline can leave us either cowering around this invitation to repentance or keeping it firmly at arm's length. We anthropomorphize God, painting Him in the image of our attachment caregiver. When called to repentance, we see our dad's angry face, a mask over God's determined love. We see our mother's disappointment. Some of us have a trauma response to conviction, similar to conflict avoidance. We are terrified as our flaws come to light. We're afraid we will be "found out," and God will pounce in anger. We fear the switch, the wooden spoon, the "board" of education.

We fear emotional abandonment.

We can't imagine that there's healing within the invitation to repentance. We can't imagine the kindness of the One desiring to unbind us.

Sometimes grief dissolves into shame, and we crawl into ourselves to a place where Love's light cannot penetrate. We're so eaten away by shame, we can't hear God's words as they come: "Comfort, comfort my people, says your God. Speak tenderly to Jerusalem, and cry to her that her warfare is ended, that her iniquity is pardoned" (Isa. 40:1–2 ESV).

Some of us experienced abuse around discipline in childhood. Punishment that went too far. Rupture that never found repair. Some experienced neglect, parents who didn't create the boundaries needed for thriving.

So, I want you to ask yourself these questions:

What did discipline look like in my family of origin?
What was a common reaction of my mother or my father when I did something wrong?
Was I over-disciplined? Was I punished for things that did not deserve the treatment I was given?
Was there repair?
How did I feel as I was punished? How did I feel afterwards?

Our attachment pain is wrapped up in this uncertainty.

Often we were taught that our attachment bond was contingent on perfect behavior. We feared isolation and disconnection every time our behavior warranted discipline and boundaries.

What if you knew God convicting you of sin was based in His abundant love, His kindness to unbind you? Remember, God's goodness and love pursuing us in Psalm 23? The Hebrew word *radaph*, translated in verse 6 as "follow," means to pursue or chase down and is used throughout the Old Testament to indicate military pursuit.[2] The psalmist uses it to illustrate God's singlemindedness in pursuing us with His goodness and mercy. The point? God's love is never neglectful. He desires you to be free because He desires you to be fully His.

The Voice translation renders Proverbs 3:11–12 in the following way, a sentiment that is later echoed in Hebrews 12:5–6.

> My son, do not ignore the Eternal's instruction
>   or lose heart when He steps in to correct you;
> Because the Eternal proves His love by *caring enough to*
>   *discipline you*,
>   just as a father does his child, his *pride and* joy.

Again, we struggle as we place our experience of discipline over the truth of God's loving character. Remember, He knows we are but dust. Our sin does not surprise God, but He wants to free us from its prison.

Sometimes the Lord's work feels uncomfortable, like a bright light or the surgeon's knife. We fear the grief of awareness. We fear we will be swallowed up by the shame.

And other times God's invitation to repentance is accompanied by vicious lies from the enemy like these: "You will never get this right." "You have hurt them beyond repair." "They will abandon you, and they will be right to do so."

These shame messages become normalized, so much so that we barely recognize their presence, though the evil one loves to spew them as a part of his destructive campaign. As we look at the way we accept or reject discipline, we can start to hear the evil one's vindictive words. We need to become awake and wise to his evil plan. Lies can get wired into our neuropathways and co-opt the beautiful rescue plan of God.

The next time you become aware of your sin, view it as the Holy Spirit leading you into new territory, a new healing. He wants to stake the cross in a previously hidden area of your life. You and He are doing this hard work together. A call to repentance is the invitation of Love to gain new ground in the rank corners of your heart.

The more attached we are to God, the more we sense an invitation to be curious with Him over our sin. Where did this come from? Is this coming from a bigger, unhealed story? We feel grief over our sin, the brokenness of relationship, the recognition that we've caused harm to others or ourself. We recognize where we've agreed with neglect, the soft indulgent whisper of easy. But now we feel God's compassion with the pain our sin has caused.

I love the NIV translation of Isaiah 51:14: "The cowering prisoners will soon be set free; they will not die in their dungeon, nor will they lack bread."

Emmanuel Stays

The accusers held stones, threatening and angry. And in response to Jesus's compassionate authority, one at a time, they dropped them, making dull thuds on the packed sand at their feet. Self-righteousness closes us to the pain in another's story, but Jesus saw the sin in their desire for punishment, their desire to wipe out another's life. They saw the woman as a threat. They did not see her wild pain as she scratched for love and attention. Adultery is often a response to attachment pain, a need to be seen. A need to be known.

Jesus stayed as they slowly abandoned the rocks in their hands, recognizing their own harbored sin. He stayed, his fingers writing in the sand. What truth do you think Emmanuel was spelling out?

As He wrote in the sand, He maintained a firm, non-anxious presence in the face of mob violence. He stayed. Her sin didn't cause

Him to turn away but to turn toward, compassion wrapping its arms around her and holding her tight.

If He *had* turned and made a quick getaway, would she have had the internal strength to "go and sin no more"? Rejection could have sent her straight back into her lover's arms. Instead, she found a man who fought for her soul, whose presence shattered the shame of being found out. She discovered gentleness, and it gave her the strength to stand in the grief of remorse as well as separation.[3]

We can have compassion on ourselves and the places where we are still bound, because Jesus showed us the way His compassion *stays* through our shame. The prodigal went searching and clawing for a life he hoped would assuage his feelings of joyless insignificance, guzzling wine and rich foods in an attempt to feed the little boy inside who craved belonging.

The father stayed on the road of his life, searching the horizon. He stayed, even as the prodigal son ran. Abandonment was never an option.

Our Abba is the one who stays. We are the ones who run.

When we believe God abandons us in our sin, we believe we are left without help. We despair and lean on willpower, something that shifts with the changing tides of our moods. Obviously, Paul felt the same way. "For I do not do the good I want to do, but the evil I do not want to do—this I keep on doing," he moaned, echoing our own personal experience (Rom. 7:19).

Brother Lawrence, after sinning, "simply acknowledged his fault and said to God: 'I shall never do otherwise if You leave me to myself; it is up to You to keep me from falling and to correct what is wrong.'"[4]

We get it. Brother Lawrence describes what we see in our mirror. We desperately need the Holy Spirit. We get caught in the net of a disastrous personal reno project, but humility is coming to the end of ourselves, the end of our own methods, the end of our willpower.

Ezekiel 11 says this, "They will return. . . . I will give them an undivided heart and put a new spirit in them; I will remove from them their heart of stone and give them a heart of flesh. Then they will follow my decrees and be careful to keep my laws. They will be my people, and I will be their God" (vv. 18, 19–20).

Their job was to return, just like the prodigal. He says His job is this:

- to give them an undivided heart
- to put a new spirit in them
- to remove their heart of stone
- to give them a heart of flesh

We think we need to take a chisel and hammer to our own heart of stone. We believe willpower will save us. Perhaps, we think, we're trying to make God's job easier, but instead, we sputter with our attempts.

Only God can transform. Only God can deliver.

It is the Holy Spirit who rolls away stones, who raises the dead. Ephesians 1:18–20 says, *"I pray that the eyes of your heart may be enlightened in order that you may know* . . . his incomparably great power for us who believe. That power is the same as the mighty strength he exerted when he raised Christ from the dead and seated him at his right hand in the heavenly realms" (emphasis added).

And again in Romans: "The [*same*] Spirit of God, who raised Jesus from the dead, lives in you. And just as God raised Christ Jesus from the dead, he will give life to your mortal bodies by this same Spirit living within you" (8:11 NLT).

The *same Spirit* who raised Christ from the dead. The same.

Perhaps in order to hollow ourselves of ego, to have room for a rush of the wind of the Spirit, we must recognize our need. We must kneel.

The Kind Chisel of God

When I think of placing myself in the Emmanuel's hands, I think of Michelangelo's prisoners or slaves in the Accademia, a museum in

Florence. They greeted us as we walked in the door. The *David* stood alone in the almost chapel-like atrium, drawing all the attention of the crowd, but it was the prisoners, four half-finished figures, who captivated my attention. There's a startling beauty in the half done, a startling beauty in the becoming. I wanted to run my hand over the unfinished, pocked marble. Atlas's body emerges from the stone, smooth arms and legs, smooth torso, but his head is thrown back, his face still encased in marble, still concealed. Was Michelangelo ever going to come back to finish them? No one knows.

They're in various stages of completion, and every time I see them, I have a feeling of kinship. I get discouraged with my own becoming, the half-finished and pockmarked heart, the crusty and the caustic, the half-healed wounds that, when touched, still jump up and surprise me with their ferocious yelp. I'm still emerging. I'm messy, and at times, I am thoroughly disheartened. I either double-down, trying to transform myself, or I isolate with depression.

Repentance is submitting to the kind chisel of God.

We believe we need to take a chisel and hammer to ourselves, but it's God who has final glorious art in His mind.

Spiritual director and enneagram coach Marilyn Vancil wrote,

> We don't have to stress and strain to be restored; our work is to be-lieve and surrender to God's guidance and life-giving love. We don't have to "dig up stuff"; God will show us where and what needs heal-ing. We don't have to fear God's restoration project; God is not out to get us, but to reclaim our original design.[5]

We scrape and scratch at our shadow side with a giant loofah when all along, the thing we need is the purifying light of our res-urrected Christ. We need God to walk beside us as we get curi-ous and ask Him why we're reacting with such vicious force when we're triggered. We need God's wisdom at the place of our deepest wounding. If our story encounters the resurrection power of Christ, the sin infection that would have seeped out of our wounds will no longer spread. Through *our* future. Through the future of the next generation.

————

Let's get practical. In the extra videos included at summerjoygr oss.com/the-emmanuel-promise, I'll lead you in the 7 R's of repentance as well as a Lectio Divina of Exodus 34:6.

14

Lectio Divina

Slowing the Word to Hear His Voice

Definition: Lectio Divina is a prayerful and relational reading of Scripture. It's an ancient prayer practice in which we meditate on a short section of text through repetition, allowing it to transform us.

Attachment Principle: Through Lectio Divina, the Spirit uses the "God-breathed" Word of God as healing balm on our attachment wounds, revealing Himself as perfect caregiver and exchanging our toxic lies for the truth that we are His beloved children.

Scripture: "Let the word of Christ dwell in you richly" (Col. 3:16 ESV). "For the word of God is living and active, sharper than any two-edged sword, piercing to the division of soul and of spirit, of joints and of marrow, and discerning the thoughts and intentions of the heart" (Heb. 4:12 ESV).

How to Pray Lectio Divina

1. Pick a small passage of Scripture, five verses or less.
2. Begin by quieting, opening yourself to the present moment, bringing your ruminating mind to stillness. Asking God to control your thinking and be your teacher.

3. Then listen as you read the text. Once. Twice. Three times. It's in the repetition that you allow the seed of the Word to go deeper.

4. Consider what words or phrases are asking for attention. Bring your present story to the edges of the Word. Sit in silence, then ask, *Lord, what is it You want me to hear?*

5. Based on this Scripture, ask, *God, do You have an invitation to know something, to do, or to become?* Again, sit in silence.

6. Finally, pray. Let your stirred emotions rise before Him. Then rest. Rest with God bookends Lectio Divina. Just enjoy togetherness. Perhaps take a word from the text and breathe with it. Perhaps just fall silent.[1]

I grew up winning Awana badges for Scripture memorization and doing Bible quiz bowl in Sunday school rooms lit with fluorescent lights. I grew up winning points for Bible knowledge and fed off the kudos.

I'm grateful for the words I gathered there, but it took me a long time to stop using Scripture as a means to win a prize, a performance, or guardrails to keep me safely between the lines. Even wisdom can be used as a weapon, a way to control our world, to create safety. We feel vulnerable and keep people at arm's length with wisdom, dissecting people with an enneagram number or using knowledge to hold people in their place. We size people up with the credentials that follow their name. On Instagram, tiny quips of wisdom have become the currency to win followers. Instead of using the Word to transform the world, we use it as capital for platform building.

Now, stripped of prizes and performance, I'm grateful for the gift of my background and how quickly I can track a Scripture, but mostly I'm grateful for how quickly the Spirit can use a Scripture to track me. The attachment practice of Lectio Divina has made Scripture a spacious place to meet with my Emmanuel. Each word becomes weighty as I become awake and aware that the One who authored and inspired the Word is present in the room with me.

By slowly reading Scripture in the presence of our Emmanuel, we begin to memorize the tone of His voice. I open the covers of the Word and, together, we look at His story from Genesis through Revelation. As I open the Gospels, I gather the privilege of His intimate self-revelation. Just like the first days of dating, when Andrew and I asked each other our stories, in Scripture, God's character is slowly revealed, and I can't get enough. I'm awed. This is the One who is captain of angel armies? *This* is the One who has pursued me to the cross? *Emmanuel, show me more. Show me who You are.* Lectio Divina is a relational reading of the Word. As we slow down the Word, His story becomes even more tender. His words are wound around our years, and over time we are grafted into His redemption story.

Lectio Divina invites us to come to the Word, not as a conqueror but with openness and expectancy. But openness is never passive; it's active. Just think—before the soil is ready, it is rent. Clods broken up. Nutrients mixed in. There's a tilling. We are actively opening to the Word by choosing to come with our hearts bare and vulnerable.

By taking deep breaths or quieting our nervous system through grounding, we are actively choosing to become good soil, ready for the seed of the Word. We are opening to connection, not just information. We are choosing transformation, not just the checking off of a to-do list.

Lectio Divina at Work

It all started when I read Psalm 139 one night before falling asleep. I went to my room with a steaming mug of chamomile tea. I mulled it over in my mouth, breathing in its earthy fragrance and then licking the honey resting at the bottom. I stopped reading abruptly on verse 14, and at first the words seemed embarrassingly forthright, prideful even: "fearfully and wonderfully made." It felt like I was reading about breasts in the Song of Solomon. Inappropriate. Overly intimate. But I kept chewing over these words, knowing there was a truth I was dodging. Finally, I fell asleep.

All through the night "fearfully and wonderfully made" wound its way through my dreams and then reappeared with the first light of morning. Repetition had stripped the verse of the false veneer of pride. I turned the Scripture over and over like a key in my hand, as if it were a foreign object I'd searched for and began to feel *delighted* by what God had said. I was Mary Lennox, holding the key to the secret garden.

I was around Mary's age, ten, when I lost sight of God's delight in me, when I forgot what "fearfully and wonderfully made" meant. I loved words and music, color and theater. Those around me had their own art. Layups and effortless play. They had the art of a woven-in community. They were tall. Thin. I looked completely different. Short. Curvy. I felt awkward and *different*. Was I also somehow misshapen? This was the lie I conjured up to try to understand my world.

Trauma Creates Lies

Lies squeeze our world into dark little labyrinths, where it becomes impossible to find our way out on our own. Most of the time the lies are subconscious, but they dim the lights on our life, and we don't even realize we've made an agreement with the underworld.

It's natural. Lies form as a way to make sense of the life being thrown our direction. Our brains naturally attempt to put together disparate pieces of a puzzle to make meaning. They are trying to understand the world, manufacturing a lie where there's only an open-ended series of lived stories.

After four years of people pleasing and trying to belong, I had walked the neural pathway of "I will always be rejected" so many times, it had worn a path that all other thoughts followed along. Lies are uncreative and surprisingly monotonous and yet, at the same time, they can be deeply personal and particular.

Here are other situations where a lie is created that a child might grab on to:

Their parents divorce and they believe it must have been their fault. *They won't fight for me. I must have something wrong inside me.* And/or *I have been abandoned. I will always be abandoned.*

A child experiences sexual abuse and, in vulnerability, every lie thrown their direction sticks like darts on a dartboard. *It's my fault. I liked it. I made them do this. No one will believe me. My life will fall down around me like a pile of bricks if I tell someone.*

Sometimes lies are created through meaning-making. Sometimes they are spoken out loud and consumed all at once. Sometimes they can be silent, inferred but no less powerful.

Your mother was taken away because God needed her more. Or *You must have been adopted because you don't fit.*

And we can't forget the uncreative classics, like, *You're not as smart as your sister ... You're not pretty ... You'll never measure up ... You will never belong.*

Lies are all predictable variations on an evil theme whispered ad nauseum—until they are confronted with truth. "He sent out his word and healed them; he rescued them from the grave" (Ps. 107:20). Until the lie comes out of the subconscious, ready for transformation, it festers and becomes gangrenous. Until the lie meets Emmanuel's presence, the Word written and the Word incarnate, it will be easily aggravated and spread.

Emmanuel Untangles the Lie

Emmanuel is always speaking life. And, Dear One, when Scripture shines a spotlight on a different Scripture that uproots a rooted lie, hold on tight. This is the beginning of your untangling. Sometimes when you encounter that Scripture, you feel like a cat basking in the warmth of a sunbeam. You want to lay down and spread out and never leave. Sometimes, like with the Psalm 139 passage, it feels awkward, embarrassing, or prideful. You think that word must be for someone else. The old log in the eye bit. This is a key. Pay attention. All Scripture was made "for teaching, rebuking, correcting and training in righteousness, so that the servant of God may be thoroughly equipped for every good work" (2 Tim. 3:16–17). If you think a word was written for another hearer, pay closer attention.

"I praise you, for I am fearfully and wonderfully made" felt just like that (Ps. 139:14 ESV). It confronted the shadow of rejection by throwing direct light at it, but at first, it felt off. *This can't possibly be for me*, I thought. The tired lie had been whispering, "You're different. You walk in the world wonky." And "I praise you, for I am fearfully and wonderfully made" spoke of God's purpose in creating individual joys all wrapped up in skin. His making is never a mistake.

Later on that day, I went to the fitness center and, after working out, found a quiet room while my children played with others. I opened the Scripture back up. The key was already in the verse! "I praise you, for I am fearfully and wonderfully made." Praise! Could I possibly praise God for the way I was created? Could I lift an offering of rising gratefulness?

Sometime before that morning, I had started accepting the imperfect gifts of each day, thanking God. Instead of sinking in shame, I tried to lift each "failed" interaction up, asking Him to bless and fill them with His resurrection power, to redeem rejection and write a different story. So why couldn't I do that with myself?

Yes, I am imperfect. I will always be imperfect, but my continued anger at myself and the story that created me was not making matters easier. Could I not only accept God's gift of me but also lift up my arms and praise Him?

Fearfully and Wonderfully Made

One Sunday evening, heavy summer sun invited us west to the Lake Michigan shore. As soon as we hit the sand, my kids scattered, all dressed in red swimsuits, and I tipped my face to the sun, turning my ear to listen.

Summer, thank Me, I heard.

Instead of sitting on our blanket with a book, my normal modus operandi, I began to play too. I pushed around rocks stuck deep at the water's edge and occasionally I glanced up. I could hear my husband's deep laugh as he helped five-year old Madeline balance her boogie board on the waves.

God, help me, too, to learn balance and to love me, because not loving me is creating a dam of my life, truncating my ability to open my arms wide.

As I pushed the large rocks around the wet sand, forming a cross, the voice of God became clear. I listened: *Summer Joy, whose authority will you accept as true? The junior high girls from your past or the God of the universe?* The question seemed a bit ludicrous. "I praise you because I am fearfully and wonderfully made" comes straight from Scripture and who was I to question the God of the universe's authority? He is the Light of the World, so why would I study the carnival mirror someone else set before me?

I stood on the flat rock at the center of the cross and lifted my arms up to the sky. *Who am I not to thank You for the gift that You have given, to refuse any gift from You? Bless the Lord O my soul and all that is within me, and so I lift up my fullness and my emptiness, my imperfections and my gifts.*

The Roman Catholic priest Romano Guardini writes words that invite me to open the gift in his essay, "The Acceptance of Oneself": "The act of self-acceptance is the root of all things. I must agree to be the person who I am. Agree to the qualifications which I have. Agree to live within my limits. The clarity and the courageousness of this acceptance is the foundation of all existence."[2]

The beach had emptied for dinnertime, and I stood, balancing on this rock cross, arms up. I prayed, *You loved me even while I was a sinner. And if You with Your pierced hands can accept me, then who am I not to accept the gift?*

And if I was a gift, so was the precious little one who toddled up in her bathing suit covered with red cherries, splashing through the puddle beside the cross. I looked into her tanned face with the four new serrated white teeth and told her that she, too, was a gift of God. She kept coming back for more attention through the rest of the evening, eyes wide, drinking love.

This is why this self-acceptance, this thanksgiving, is the opposite of pride. Being a gift does not mean the least of these is not. Being filled with this thanksgiving makes me want to go out into the highways and byways and put faces in my hands and speak truth into dry hearts. "You," teenager with the hungry, aching eyes, "are fearfully and wonderfully made."

As we left the beach that day, I wanted to whisper it into the heart of everyone I saw. On the way home I told the cashier at the grocery store with the lovely lips and the dreary store coat, "I hope you know that you are lovely." She smiled and a light turned on in those almond-shaped eyes just for a moment.

Don't Hurry the Healer

When we're in a hurry to get to the next thing, to close our Bible, grab our coat, and rush out the door, we rush right past transformation. Only when we linger with the Word do its seeds have a fighting chance to take root. We are transformed as we hold on to the Word tightly. There's a quickening within us. We get curious. *Why does this Word feel so profound, Lord? What are You trying to say?*

We hold on to the hem of the Healer, the Word always present. Hold. Hold. Hold. Healing occurs in determined perseverance. It's all over the New Testament. The blind man crying out to Jesus as He passes by. The friend who knocks with shameless persistence. The Canaanite woman not taking no for an answer if it means going back to her daughter, still twisting in pain.

Faith rises not because we've conjured a feeling of it, but because we are determined to stay present. "You are here," we state. "You have what I need." Author and nun Macrina Wiederkehr explains it this way: "The reason we live so dimly and with such divided hearts is that we have never really learned how to be present with quality to God, to self, to others. . . . We meet all of these lovely gifts only half there. Presence is what we are all starving for."[3]

Be Expectant of Emmanuel

"Greetings, you who are highly favored. The Lord is with you." If the bright light wasn't enough to send Mary's knees straight to the ground, these words would.

She may have thought that, as a young girl barely picked out for engagement, she was hidden away in a small village. But Gabriel was naming her. "Highly favored: God takes joy in you." Can you see her shaking her head, unable to receive those words? Then Gabriel said, "The Lord is with you." It was a statement of fact, as true then as it is in the room with you now.

"How?" she asked. His answer? She would be overshadowed by the Holy Spirit. The same Spirit who suspended over the waters in creation would hover over her.

Isn't that what we all need? The Spirit hovering. Genesis 1:2–like.

I love this part of the exchange. After Gabriel spoke: "No word from God will ever fail," Mary gave her consent through reiterating that same statement. "I am the Lord's servant. Let Your Word have its way with me."

I'm taking liberties with this text from Luke 1:26–38. But that's essentially what Mary was saying, "Let Your Word have its way with me." This was trust, openhearted vulnerability. Expectancy. Mary became expectant through expectancy.

I wonder if this can be our prayer as well whenever we open the sacred text. "I am the Lord's servant. Let Your Word have its way with me."

Reverse the Trend

Technology and the way we are consuming information is resculpting our brains. It's slicing and dicing our attention span.

In an article titled "The Death of Reading Is Threatening the Soul," prolific author Philip Yancey confessed to an internal pull to skim, to jump from article to article, to alight on quotes instead of immersing himself between the covers of longer books.[4]

I'm recognizing this same shift in myself. I have the bizarre tendency to go from amazing quote to amazing quote on Instagram and skim like I'm trying to make a satisfying meal out of a buffet of cucumber sandwiches and petit fours. I have the sugar rush to prove it.

The slow feast of Lectio Divina can be an awkward practice at first, sitting with a Scripture not packaged in a tweet. We are used to immediate emotional connectivity—someone curating a quote that has the potential to go viral. We are accustomed to the jolt, the effortless aha moment. If we're not careful, we will be building our home in the shallows, as Nicholas Carr expertly points out in his Pulitzer Prize finalist book, *The Shallows*.

In Lectio Divina we learn to pause, to linger, to listen. We learn to pull out a chair for the Author, the Main Character, the One who holds the story together. Then, just as in the post-resurrection story of the two grieving disciples on their way to Emmaus, through Lectio Divina, Jesus breaks open the bread, and we grow silent in wonder as we realize how much we've missed Him.[5]

OK, let's dive in. In the corresponding videos for this chapter at summerjoygross.com/the-emmanuel-promise, we will savor God's Word in Isaiah 55. You'll also find a free Lectio Divina worksheet for you or your group to use.

16

The 3 R's

Saturated by Love

Definition: The 3 R's—Rest, Receive, and Respond—is a contemplative practice that grounds us in God's presence through rest and invites us to receive and linger in an encounter of His love before we respond out of spontaneous gratitude.

Attachment Principle: As our nervous system is quieted in love through an encounter with God, we begin to build a database of memories with our Abba Father.

Scripture: "See what great love the Father has lavished on us, that we should be called children of God! And that is what we are!" (1 John 3:1).

How to Pray the 3 R's

Rest: We take deep breaths and ground our bodies. This is how we open our arms to receive.

Receive: We ask for an image or a memory of God loving us, focusing on each sense in the image.

Respond: We spontaneously respond with loving gratitude.

It's time to wake up to the powerful, life-transforming attachment love of your Abba. It's time for your nervous system to learn to rest in Divine Love.

Have you ever seen a toddler trying to wake from night terrors—hair covered with sweat, head shaking, arms reaching, eyes darting back and forth? They are still living the reality of their nightmare. My oldest would scream, eyes open, as if he was still seeing the ghosts that haunted his sleep. He looked awake, but he was still stuck in the quicksand of his bad dream. In his twisting and turning, I struggled to keep him safe from his own thrashing. I took him in my arms, rocked him, sang to him, and held him tight until his body began to rest in my arms.

When children awake from nightmares, their nervous system has to be convinced that there is another story that is more true. Sometimes this calming requires just a few minutes of comforting. Sometimes it takes much longer.

I wonder how much of our lives are spent stuck in the waking nightmare of a lie. With triggers stemming from our original attachment relationship, we get stuck in a story of abandonment, of scarcity, and of pursuing powers gaining ground. These lies convince us we've been forsaken, and our God is powerless to save us. Dear One, this has never been your true reality. You have been adopted by the One who holds the power of the universe. By the One who declared to Moses that He is "The LORD, the LORD, the compassionate and gracious God, slow to anger, abounding in love and faithfulness" (Exod. 34:6). Your story is being written with the pen of Divine Love.

In order for you to receive an earned secure attachment with your Abba, you need to believe the truth of your new reality as a beloved child. You are invited to rest in Divine Love, not just believe it exists somewhere in the ether.

The practice in this chapter, the 3 R's, is one of the simplest and most profound ways to retrain the nervous system to believe you are safe in the loving arms of God.

A Simple but Not Simplistic Practice

After ten years in the lakeside community of South Haven, Andrew and I discerned it was time to move, to walk with a new community. He was to be the head pastor of a church in a mining town in central Pennsylvania where his family had roots. It was late May when we packed the U-Haul, looking forward to the new adventure. In preparation, we had rented out our yellow cottage in South Haven to vacationers.

As the last box was being taped up, there was a phone call. There had been a misunderstanding, we were told. The new job was no longer ours.

Can you feel the magnitude of my internal earthquake? We unpacked at my mom and dad's house in eastern Pennsylvania, unsure of where we would eventually land. Over the next few months, I had literal nightmares as my brain tried to reconcile this bizarre new reality. Andrew set up an office in the basement where he began creating websites, memorizing code, and perusing job sites. The earth kept shifting under our feet. Would we find a church? What was "stable"? During this tumultuous season, I learned the power of the 3 R's, a practice Terry Wardle later expounded on in the profound little book *Every Breath We Take*, where he mapped it out further.[1]

It is a generous practice that can fit easily in the time you have to give it. It can take two minutes while standing in the checkout line or it can take fifteen minutes while you linger. You can do it alone, sitting with your morning tea, or you can do it in a group, with each person's experience multiplying your joy.

Perfect Love Drives Out Fear

Rest is the quieting of our nervous system. Deep breaths. We are grounding our nervous system and saying yes to being fully *with* God. Our thrashing is stilled. Slowly we become available to connection. Again, our nervous system has to be convinced we are safe to rest in God's presence in order for attachment to be built.

In *Receive*, we ask God for an image of His love for us. It's a 3D polaroid slowly developing. What do we see in that image? What do we hear? What does our skin feel? Is there anything we smell or taste?

Remember, attachment is created through the experience of the senses. It's built one slow gaze, one smile, one tender touch on the shoulder, one message of warmth and care at a time.

As a spiritual director, I sometimes ask people to remember a time when they felt loved by God, and we enter back into that story with our senses. This walking around in a memory of loving care reinforces the original message and the neural pathway of attachment—love is deepened. The gift is unwrapped again, reinforcing the true story of God's nearness, His comfort, love, and care.

As we know from trauma specialists, when someone remembers a traumatic incident, they have all the emotions and experiences of the original trauma within the memory. Their body remembers it as if they are back in that moment. In fact, they often reexperience the same overwhelming emotions.

The corresponding truth is that as someone remembers a moment of joy or love, the original experience of warmth rushes over them and they reexperience that beautiful moment. Love is reinforced. They walk around in it.

Here are a few other ways to receive:

Ask Jesus to give you a picture of where He is in the room and how He is loving you right here, right now.[2]

Invite your Abba to give you a picture of Him inviting you to "be still, and know that [He is] God" (Ps. 46:10).

Request that God would show you an image of Him quieting you with His love (see Zeph. 3:17 ESV).

Then, friend, as I've said before, stay right there. Linger. Soak it in. In order to build new neuropathways, we have to stay in the reality of this sensory-packed encounter with our Emmanuel for thirty seconds to three minutes. Our nervous system has to be convinced that there is another story that is more true.

Respond is simple but, again, not simplistic. Tell Him how you feel. We say "I love you too" or "thank you" or express gratitude in a hundred different yet personal ways. Responding to God keeps us from being a consumer of God. We are in a relationship, and relationships go back and forth. Receiving love. Giving love. Receiving. Giving.

As you receive this gift of God's love from His generous heart, you run back into His arms, declaring, "Thank You, Abba!" And His heart swells with joy because *you* are His joy.

With each prayer session, engaging this simple but profound practice, you are building memories of a life infused with attachment love and experiencing a nervous system quieted in the arms of God. Come awake, Dear One. The nightmare is over. You are invited to live in the open embrace of your Abba, the King.

Love is your new reality.

————

Still wondering how the 3 R's works? No problem. Let's learn together. You can push play on a video where I lead you through the 3 R's at summerjoygross.com/the-emmanuel-promise. You'll also find a Lectio Divina video leading you in a prayer time with 1 John 3:1.

16

Breath Prayer

Resting in God

Definition: Breath prayer is a simple contemplative prayer that builds muscle memory as we abide with God through both the calm of ordinary days and the roughest of life's hurricanes. It is a simple way to shut off the sympathetic nervous system and come to a place of rest in the presence of your Emmanuel.

Attachment Principle: When we marry Scripture or a prayer phrase with our breath, we experience being quieted in God's love (see Zeph. 3:17 ESV). It's a simple attachment practice that can be easily woven through our day.

Scripture: "You keep him in perfect peace whose mind is stayed on you, because he trusts in you" (Isa. 26:3 ESV).

Two Forms of Breath Prayer

Simple Breath Prayer: Take four or five deep breaths, extending your exhale. Inhale a phrase of Scripture. Exhale the same phrase or a continuation of it. Here's an example: (inhale)

The Lord (exhale) *is my shepherd.* Or the classic prayer: (inhale) *Lord Jesus Christ* (exhale) *Son of God,* (inhale) *Have mercy on me* (exhale) *a sinner.*

Centering Prayer: Set a timer for anywhere between five minutes and twenty minutes, then breathe in and out with a word or short phrase, "centering" your attention on communion with God. Every time your attention wanders, gently bring your mind back to the word or phrase. Your mind will begin to still in the presence of God. Author Brendan Manning invites us to pray, "Abba Father, I belong to you" in order to build attachment with God,[1] and I pray the simple words, *held* and *beloved* or just *Yours.* You will discover your own.

Where is Jesus in the midst of our suffering and how can we grasp on to the hand of our Emmanuel as we walk through the fire?

Many people are asking the wrong question. They ask, "How can I avoid or escape suffering?" It's a human question. Even Jesus showed His humanity by wrestling with coming suffering in the garden of Gethsemane, asking the disciples to watch and pray with Him while He contended with what God was asking of Him. Wanting to escape suffering is deeply human.

And this is what we think to ourselves, *If only I behave by linking good moral behavior to the right words and quantity of prayers, God will lift me out of this pain.* I wonder if you can hear my frustration. Many of the people I see in spiritual direction are struggling with deep disappointment in the God of the universe emanating from this immature view of life. Sometimes it's even preached from the pulpits. We have not traveled far from the book of Job.

And this is where my frustration comes from: when we espouse this formulaic idea of God as genie who can wave away our pain, we end up shaming those who are suffering instead of coming alongside them. Lord, have mercy. The suffering ones are often collateral damage from this twisted theology. And if this is you, I'm so sorry.

Your story of suffering is holy. You have not done anything wrong. And as Jesus said about the blind man in John 9:4, neither you nor your parents have sinned to create the pain you are in now. No, we are walking a sin-scarred, broken earth, and suffering is part of the air we breathe down here.

The kingdom of God is not about escaping suffering. The kingdom of God is about coming into deep, abiding communion with Jesus Christ and being transformed into His likeness, even *through* suffering.

Please don't misunderstand me. I believe in the beautiful healing touch of Jesus, but I believe victory reflects God's power back to Him, not our perfectly followed formula. Yes, prayer is powerful and we are invited into the greatest partnership on earth—on our knees. I come from a long line of intercessors and it's an honor.

But God's healing is a mystery. A glorious mystery. He loves for us to ask. He's a good Father, planning good things. And Hallelujah, yes, I've experienced healing myself. But if we could bottle the resolution ourselves, we'd try to sell it and steal the glory for ourselves.

No, Jesus put on human flesh and, despite being the Son of God, He suffered along with us.

Isaiah 53:3 says, "He was despised and rejected by mankind, a man of *suffering*, and familiar with pain" (emphasis added). And even then, the suffering was shamed. The verse goes on to describe Him: "like one from whom people hide their faces he was despised, and we held him in low esteem."

Job suffered righteously and confounded his amateur theologian friends. In these days, they would have easily been hired as Hallmark card writers, capturing all the sentiments that make us cringe when we stand in a funeral line.

Paul suffered. Paul goes as far as to say this in Romans 5:

We rejoice in our sufferings, knowing that suffering produces endurance, and endurance produces character, and character produces hope, and hope does not put us to shame, because God's love has been poured into our hearts through the Holy Spirit who has been given to us. (vv. 3–5 ESV)

Rejoice in suffering?

Paul was saying that suffering can be like a well-digging drill. We find deeper waters, new waters. Still waters.

You've seen one of those saints who radiate joy, who have a trust in God that registers as stillness? More than likely that person has suffered. Deeply. You can read their story in the scars on their bodies, but their souls look a whole lot like Jesus.

They were ravaged by the storm and clung to the hand of Jesus. And they're still clinging to His hand when they walk out the other side.

Isaiah 43:2 says, "When you pass through the waters, I will be with you; and when you pass through the rivers, they will not sweep over you. When you walk through the fire, you will not be burned; the flames will not set you ablaze."

The operative word here is *when*. When you suffer. And His answer is, "I will be with you."

The question is, Where is Jesus in the midst of our pain? Before He ascended, He said, "I am with you always, to the very end of the age" (Matt. 28:20). And last words have a way of echoing in the later silence. "I will be with you always" echoes through the centuries.

The question is, Jesus, would You show me a picture of how You desire to be with me in the midst of my present suffering?

We practice gazing into the eyes of Jesus on the good days so that when the bad days come, we can ride the waves of pain while locked on to His gaze. Sometimes our bodies teach our minds to pray. We kneel to confess. We bow our heads in humility. We raise our arms to proclaim a great bodily YES to our God during worship. We hold out our hands, palms up, to show God and our own hearts a posture of receptivity.

And when we're going through waves of grief or physical pain, we need muscle memory to walk with the One who is always walking *with* us. Breath prayer helps us build the spiritual muscle to do just that.

Riding Out Pain

All my labors were long. The first was thirty-two hours. It was Michigan and late December, but it was mild that day. I buttoned my peacoat over my pregnant belly and Andrew drove us out to the lighthouse where we walked the beach. I stopped every so often stilled by pain, closing my eyes, feeling the slow work of my body. Breathing.

I was convinced pain meds would rob us of our early bonding with our new arrival, so Andrew looked into my eyes during waves of contractions and retold the stories of our travels pre-children:

- The great wall of China and the long view down the valleys
- The mission trip to Tibet and walking into the Potala Palace, the smell of yak fat candles
- The Buddhist monk wrapped in orange who invited us into his cell and offered us Tang, flicking out a fly when he thought we weren't looking
- The meal at the bishop's house in Myanmar, where we were passed a plate piled with squares of clear jelly—only it wasn't jelly, it was fat from an unidentified animal.
- The backpacking tent we set up in front of the waterfall three days into a hike through Linville Gorge, North Carolina, where someone else had left a makeshift cross in the pebbles
- The trip down the Yellowstone River, where we found the only class 3 rapids on the river and popped out the other side, wet but laughing

I breathed. *Lord Jesus Christ. Son of God. Have mercy on me a sinner.* The classic breath prayer. Sometimes to myself. Sometimes out loud.

These words were the lifeboat to ride out the contractions. I had practiced praying with them for years. I pushed close to God through the words, and Andrew's eyes were the anchor. He was the hands and feet and eyes of God to get me through the waves of pain. Thirty-two hours later, I was gazing into the eyes of my newborn.

Breathing Together

The first summer of seminary, I put my arms through the sleeves of a borrowed lab coat, pinned a name badge on my pocket, and walked in and out of patient rooms washing my hands at the door and carrying a small Bible. I was doing a credit of clinical pastoral education at Duke Medical Center. Andrew and I both were. He served in the pediatric intensive care unit. I was in the neurology department on the fifth floor. I remember how inept I felt in the face of suffering.

Over that summer I memorized all the verses to "Great Is Thy Faithfulness" and "It Is Well with My Soul" and often sang them while leading a group or singing someone to sleep. And almost daily I sat with families whose loved ones were taking their last breaths. It was holy.

There were Baptist missionaries to Papua New Guinea in the corner room. The wife had a brain aneurysm, and her husband was sitting in the darkness waiting. No, they didn't want prayer.

There was a family who would pull me into their tight prayer circle to join them in their laments, moving organically from shouting to singing lines from gospel music and back, everybody bouncing up on their toes.

Then there was a woman with short red hair like my grandmother's who had come in with brain cancer for the second time. When I first looked at her chart, it was as thick as a dictionary. When I walked through her door every day, she'd ask me to sit down. I'd scoot my chair up to her bed and we would do centering prayer to the first line of Psalm 23. We'd repeat "The Lord" while slowly breathing in and "is my shepherd" while breathing out. She couldn't do the breath prayer by herself, but she could steady her breath to mine. She could lean against my prayers and find herself steadied. "Please come back tomorrow," she'd say as she held on to my hands and looked into my eyes.

I was taught centering prayer by a chaplain who had walked those same halls for fifteen years. He said the neuroscientists at Duke had wired him up and watched his brain during centering prayer. They found that a fifteen-minute prayer session was as effective as two hours of sleep.

If our simple, truncated version of breath prayer is a good way to start, centering prayer is a fifteen- or twenty-minute invitation to teach us to rest in God, gazing at the One who is gazing at us.

The chaplain said that centering prayer was a boat we could offer to help the patients ride out waves of pain.

I asked the lovely people on the Presence Project Facebook page this question, Any thoughts from those of you who have used breath prayer through hard seasons?

First, Carie had this to say about the importance of breath prayer during ordinary moments:

> Breath prayer aids me in turning and re-turning to the Lord IN THE MIDST of the dailies. For me, it's not so much a response to anxiety as it is a response to distraction and self-reliance. It helps because I don't need to come up with a prayer in my moment of need, but rather, can turn easily to an already-prepared response and reconnect with my Father.

Another Presence Project person agreed with Carie. She said she uses the breath prayer "Inhale: not mine. Exhale: but yours to counteract self-sufficiency."

Melodie shared how using breath prayer has helped her to connect with God's loving care in a season of deep grief:

A dear soul sister has been diagnosed with cognitive impairment. Her decline has/is taking me to the very edge of myself. Many times a day, I find myself full of grief, bringing my boatload of sorrow and fear to Jesus. I will place my own hand over my own heart, close my eyes, and adopt a posture of surrender as I breathe in and out the name of Jesus.

Lori told her story about walking through relational pain using breath prayer:

When our youngest moved out and my momma heart ached for him, I would pray, "Your will, Your way" pretty much all day long, especially when my heart was heavy.

Taliyah was gracious enough to share her hard and holy story with us:

There was one night in particular when my husband was recovering from his seizure, where I was lying in bed next to him paralyzed with fear and anxiety and felt so sick from a difficult pregnancy that I could barely move. I have never felt that physically, mentally, or emotionally miserable. I realized I had absolutely nowhere to turn for comfort than Jesus. As I breathed in, I spoke Jesus's name, and as I exhaled, I repeated, "You are good." Somehow, slowly, with every inhale and exhale, the intensity of my nausea and anxiety began to dissipate and after a few minutes, I fell asleep feeling God's presence in a more powerful way than I had ever felt it before. In a circumstance that felt anything but good, inhaling and exhaling God's goodness brought a peace and comfort I'll never forget.

Taliyah's story is a beautiful illustration of encountering God as He reveals Himself in Hebrews 13:5. Here it is in the Amplified

Version: "I WILL NEVER [under any circumstances] DESERT YOU [nor give you up nor leave you without support, nor will I in any degree leave you helpless], NOR WILL I FORSAKE *or* LET YOU DOWN *or* RELAX MY HOLD ON YOU [assuredly not]!"

This is His promise. Our Emmanuel will never relax His hold on you, even through waves of pain.

———

Want to learn more? I'll lead you through videos for both forms of breath prayer as well as Isaiah 43:1–2.

17

Silence

Detach to Reattach

Definition: Silence is carving out time to be fully attentive to God.

Attachment Principle: By carving out time for silence and solitude, we cocoon with God, allowing His voice to be loudest in our life. We slow and notice His provision. We detach in order to reattach.

Scripture: "For thus said the Lord GOD, the Holy One of Israel, 'In returning and rest you shall be saved; in quietness and in trust shall be your strength'" (Isa. 30:15 ESV).

Entering into the Practice of Silence

Daily: Find a quiet spot, perhaps outdoors where you can hear birdsong. Leave your technology inside. In the silence, focus on connection. Lean in. This is with-God time. Whisper to your Emmanuel that you're happy to be with Him and that this is His time.

Occasionally: Schedule silence into your calendar. Take a retreat. Don't put pressure on this time. Don't give it an agenda. Don't ask it to perform. The goal is spaciousness. Presence. Withness.

Reflect: Consider how you felt as you entered the time of silence. What thoughts crowded your mind? How many times did you reach for your phone if it was still on your person? What was it like to just be with God and not perform for Him? How did you feel after the time of silence? Just notice. Was it awkward and uncomfortable? Did you feel peace or joy? Did your needs find their voice?

Alison, a busy mom, has a basket of supplies ready for what she calls her mini retreats—snacks, a journal, a book or two, and art supplies. Because she has young ones, she can't always schedule these informal retreats, but as her husband takes over childcare, she throws the basket into the car and goes. Once at a quiet park, she spreads a quilt under a tree, gets out a case of watercolors, and allows the silence with God to untangle her mind.

Intentional silence, even for a mature Christian, can feel either scary or entirely superfluous, but when we make time for silence, we carve out space for transformation. *We have to detach in order to reattach to God.* Silence is swaddling ourselves away from the noise of the world where we are invited to become attached to our Abba. Whether it's a weekend retreat, or ten minutes of silence with our morning coffee, we're pushing aside outer noise and saying yes to an inner stillness where God has the chance to make Himself known.

Attachment and Cocooning

I sat in the local coffee shop and asked a friend questions about the adoption of her daughter. A plant vendor had filled the wall behind us with green. The shop smelled like coffee and chlorophyll. A bell rang every so often as someone entered, and a "Welcome!" rang out from the baristas. Every adoption family, my friend shared, has to become masters of attachment principles. She shared their strategy when they first brought their daughter home—limiting visitors, staying home as much as possible, sticking to a muted daily schedule, and choosing to be the only ones to take care of her needs. In adoption circles, this is called nesting or cocooning.[1] One of the goals of co-cooning is to mimic the forty weeks a baby spends in the womb—silent except for the gentle whoosh and heartbeat of the mother.

During this period, again known as cocooning, the adopted child learns to tune their ear to their new parents' voices. They learn sustenance comes from their new parents' hands. They spend time playing, beginning to create patterns of joy and delight in each other's presence. In the reverse, the newly adopted child bumps up against culture shock because, whether or not the child comes from another country, every family has its own culture and its own schedule and structure and values. Then, if the child comes from a story of trauma, this season of adapting to their new normal can be especially difficult.

In Hosea 2:14, when God said, "Therefore, I am now going to allure her; I will lead her into the wilderness and speak tenderly to her," He was inviting Israel to detach from old patterns of life and reattach to Him. The wilderness (or desert) is where God invited an enslaved people to become His covenant people; it's where the people of God received their attachment.

During our journey together, as we begin to desire an attachment with God, we hear this enticing invitation: "Come away, my Beloved." Our heart leaps as we let ourselves experience the resonating desire of God. As our attachment with God grows, we gain strength to turn from our own personal Egypts, all that's kept us in slavery, and step out into a new land, listening to Him call us His son or daughter. Our identity as beloved is cultivated in the silence and solitude.

Listen to God's remembrance of His time with Israel in the desert.

> When Israel was a child, I loved him,
>   and out of Egypt I called my son. . . .
> It was I who taught Ephraim to walk,
>   taking them by the arms;

> but they did not realize
>> it was I who healed them.
> I led them with cords of human kindness,
>> with ties of love.
> To them I was like one who lifts
>> a little child to the cheek,
>> and I bent down to feed them. (Hosea 11:1, 3–4)

This is attachment language. In the desert, Israel was fed by God's manna, morning after morning, and God hoped that with full bellies they would begin to believe that they could trust God's promise of continual care. In their wilderness, they slowly came awake to the One who was pursuing them to be His own. God knew that we attach to the One who feeds us.

The invitation to solitude and silence is a classic spiritual invitation. In the desert, no other voices intervene. No other voices reign. Like the Israelites leaving Egypt, we flee to a desert of solitude to detach from all that is keeping us in bondage. Moving into quiet, we begin to see all that has its grasp on us. We intentionally detach in order to have the ability to reattach.

Here's Saint Ignatius in his own words:

> The goal of our life is to live with God forever . . . our own response of love allows God's life to flow into us without limit. All the things in this world are gifts from God, presented to us so that we can know God more easily and make a return of love more readily. Our only desire and our own choice should be this: I want and I choose what better leads to the deepening of God's life in me.[2]

All that does not "allow God's life to flow into us" or lead to a "deepening of God's life in [us]" is what Ignatius called a disordered attachment. Naming our disordered attachments requires substantial discernment. This requires desert time.

The need for silence is nothing new. When Jesus was baptized in Matthew 3:17, He heard the words, "This is my Son, whom I love;

with him I am well pleased," and then immediately went out into the desert. Those words had forty days to root into His soul before He needed to go into battle armed with the truth of His identity.

The desert is often a place of internal conversion, of contending with all that's conflicting with the voice of our Emmanuel. After Elijah was called, he went out into the desert. After Paul became a Christian, he spent three years in Arabia.

After Constantine became a Christian, the Christian church went from persecuted to a fortress of power and wealth. Fathers and mothers of the church fled to the desert knowing the toll the materialism of the state-sanctioned church could take on their souls. They feared a sleepy apathy of easy Christianity. They were concerned the sudden career ladder of spiritual hierarchies would become so enticing they would lose their attachment to God; they fled to the desert to stay His. They fled to the desert to remove the temptations that were already gaining hold.

Silence is where we are converted to a life of communion. Theologian Henri Nouwen reminds us, "Solitude is not a private therapeutic place. Rather, it is the place of conversion, the place where the old self dies and the new self is born. We choose the desert to begin attuning to one voice, learning to be His child."[3]

The Revelation of Silence

Be gentle with yourself as you step into silence. Sometimes silence is a journey into the tender places of the human heart. We may feel restless, no longer disassociating with the constant availability of entertainment. In the silence, our egos step out from in front of the warped mirrors of the fun house of modern life. Our egos may feel the discomfort of being unmasked, but spiritual sobriety can ultimately lead us to receive the love we've been searching for.

Solitude and silence are often revelatory. In the quiet, the ragged state of our heart can feel exposed. Raw. Our inner longings reach for a voice. Needs long ignored, surface, and grief reminds us of its presence with a low drone. Don't worry, friend. This is the healing gift behind silence.

If we stay grounded in God's compassion, we will recognize that our Shepherd is inviting our true self, needy and wounded, to come into His presence. It's here, where we allow our ache to be seen and cherished, that the Great Physician has ample time to tend to and bandage our wound.

Presence Project member Kim described her experience with silence like this:

> Silence is one of the very best gifts I give myself again and again. For in silence I can allow my spirit to commune with God and allow my brokenness space to speak to my heart. In silence the groans surface, the wisdom comes, the anxiety settles. Silence is the place I eluded for so many years, fearing aloneness. Now I find it a very, very dear friend.

Sometimes, when we first begin to introduce silence into our lives, through a long daily walk, a weekly tech fast, or a retreat, we imagine we're doing it wrong. Instead of feeling energized and connected with God, we feel heavy and tired, depressed even. Again, this is normal. It's a part of our detox from a culture of hurry. Psalm 127:2 in the Message says, "Don't you know [God] enjoys giving rest to those he loves?" Jesus never flogged Himself for being human. When He was tired, He napped. Rest is not indulgence, it's provision. Science tells us silence is healing for our brains. It aids neurogenesis, memory, and emotional regulation.[4] Cortisol comes down. Breath deepens. We become more human.

Here's what other Presence Project members said about silence.

Deb: I like to move when I'm [practicing] silence. Labyrinth walks keep my body engaged and help silence my busy mind.

Kelly: Silence has been one of the chief ways God has been healing me from my need to produce or perform. Each day I do twenty minutes of centering prayer. I'm also learning to leave the radio off in the car when I'm alone. The true gift of silence has been coming as I am encountering the unconditional love of God.

Sindhu: Practicing silence is so hard for me as I would often rather avoid feeling alone. But I know deep down that God offers the silence that manifests as solitude (as Nouwen says) so the best way for me to practice silence is by getting my body moving.

Mary Jo: I have to do some breathwork before my body is still enough to be silent. I ask Jesus to slow me down, to gently support me. I intentionally let go of the sounds of distraction. The benefit of silence for me is a calming clarity and a deep sense of gratitude.

Kathleen: There are three ways I practice silence:
- daily, contemplative morning prayer
- hiking/walking in nature
- a yearly overnight silent retreat
  The gift of silence is wrestling through distractions in order to be comfortable just being in God's presence. I fight not to be outcome oriented.

My own favorite way to practice silence is to have a three-day retreat pendulating between solitude and togetherness. I often do this with a good friend who understands the gift of silence herself. We give order to our time, waking up and spending the day in silence, then cooking together, lighting a fire, and enjoying conversation in the evenings in the light of its glow.

The Good News

The word *silence* was written on the agenda from Wednesday evening to Thursday morning at the summer residency.[5] As the silent day approached, I felt the relief of the approaching solitude. I'm usually held captive by my to-do list. I'm usually a willing captive of my family's needs. But inside the scheduled solitude, I experienced the freedom of a beloved child.

After supper I walked to the dock of a pond and took up residence. I watched small schools of sunfish flow through the water grasses and tiny, long-nosed fish wriggle into the bottom muck, sending up a cloud and then reaching out to grasp what rose. I heard monster fish thrashing about on the pond's edge and bullfrogs croaking. Clouds streaked over the tree line to the west, and I settled in for a sunset. In the silence, I was able to be a quiet witness to God's glory.

It felt like I was capturing something incredibly indulgent and yet basic to human need. Silence is an invitation to discover the tables God has set in the wilderness. It gives us ample time to wait for His presence. We stop demanding His good gifts on our own timetable. Delight rises without requiring the prodding of entertainment. In silence, we become enamored with the tone of our Emmanuel's voice. He has less competition. We no longer crave the distance of numbing. We seek Him out with a spacious soul, no longer beating back the overwhelm that crests over our calendar days. We begin to walk secure in our belovedness.

Does silence still feel intimidating? Let's do this together. At su mmerjoygross.com/the-emmanuel-promise, you'll find resources for retreats as well as Lectio Divina videos on Hosea 2 and 11.

18

Ignatian Imaginative Prayer

Behold Him

Definition: Ignatian Imaginative Prayer (or Ignatian Contemplation) engages the senses through the holy imagination, inviting us to experience a gospel story like a movie, allowing it to unfold slowly, giving us time to encounter the living Christ.

Attachment Principle: Through the science of mirror neurons, when we encounter Jesus through the holy imagination in the Gospels, we view His character up close and we can't help but become captivated. Our skewed image of God from our attachment wound can be transformed. We watch His compassion and begin to believe that compassion is available for us.

Scripture: "Let us fix our eyes on Jesus, the author and perfecter of our faith, who for the joy set before Him endured the cross, scorning its shame, and sat down at the right hand of the throne of God" (Heb. 12:2 BSB).

Practicing Ignatian Imaginative Prayer

Pick a familiar story about Jesus from the Gospels.

Read through the story many times. Notice the sensory details.
Notice each character who makes an appearance. Who

draws your attention? What is the main conflict? How is it resolved? What is the purpose of this story?

What emotions arise in you as you read this story? Why? How does this story touch your own life situation? Be curious with God.

Now, it's time to take three to five deep breaths, to get quiet and grounded. Then, ask the Holy Spirit to anoint your imagination, heighten your senses, and guide this time of prayer.

Even before you enter the story, spend a moment gazing on the One who is gazing on you.

Then, close your eyes and allow yourself to connect to the senses in the details of the story. What do you see? Hear? Smell? Taste? Touch? Imagine you're one of the characters in the narrative. You can choose to be a main character or someone in the crowd watching. Maybe you're Peter asking Jesus to call you to walk on the water. Maybe you're another disciple in the boat.

Allow the story to unfold slowly like a movie. Take your time. Watch. Listen. Focus your attention on Jesus.

Again, get curious. What would you like to know about Jesus's experience in the story? Ask Him. Linger there with Jesus for a few minutes. Does He have a word for you? What would you like to ask Him? What would you like to tell Him about *your* story? Can you tell how He feels about you? Recognize where in the story you had a heightened emotional connection with Him. Linger in that moment. Write a few notes in a journal.

Share this experience with a safe, trusted friend, a pastor, or a spiritual director, and on your own, reread your journal, connecting with the story again. Let it soak like a seed in good ground.

I had opened my binder at a table near the middle of the conference room at Ashland Seminary in 2010, while listening to Dr. Anne

Halley of Healing Care Ministries teach on healing attachment wounds. After her teaching, she led us into an Ignatian Imaginative Prayer exercise of Jesus blessing the children. As she invited us to feel the dirt under our feet and the warmth of the sun on our face, Scripture leapt alive. Jesus, the center of the story, came alive. She invited us to imagine ourselves as small children, standing in line, watching others receive Jesus's tender attentions, then standing in front of Him ourselves, His hand on our head. Through this exercise, I was captivated by Emmanuel, His kind look focused directly at me. I didn't want to leave His presence.

When Ignatian Imaginative Prayer is done well, it's like walking onto a movie set. We walk along the shore of the Sea of Galilee, our sandals sliding over the rocks to put our toes in the edge of the water. As we listened to the caw of seagulls, our attention is drawn to the smell of fish roasting over coals. It's a humble meal, but we know we're welcome when we find Jesus behind the fire, inviting us with a fish on a stick. It's here that our appetites are whetted for more time with Jesus. It's here that we experience the beauty Hebrews only hints at, of the Word of God "alive and active. Sharper than any double-edged sword" (4:12).

Along with Holocaust survivor Corrie Ten Boom, we are surprised at how God reaches out to us through the pages of His Word. She wrote, "Sometimes I would slip the Bible from its little sack with hands that shook, so mysterious had it become to me. It was new; it had just been written. I marveled sometimes that the ink was dry."[1]

The Imagination, a Doorway for Attachment

Saint Ignatius, Saint Augustine, Saint Catherine of Siena, Julian of Norwich, Teresa of Ávila, even the early church fathers Saint Gregory of Nyssa and Saint John of Damascus taught that we can pray with images inspired by the Holy Spirit. As the Eastern Orthodox theologian Kallistos Ware argues, to dismiss the use of mental or physical images in prayer and worship is "to imply that [Christ's] body, and so his humanity, is somehow unreal."[2]

Even before that, David invited us into his own prayer of holy imagination in Psalm 23. We feel the blades of grass under our bare feet. We cup our hands in the cool water of the running stream splashing it on our faces, noting the feeling of the rod and staff at our sides, symbols of the Shepherd's protection. Psalm 23 is dripping with the senses and helps us engage the presence of God with our imagination.

Praying with the senses is punctuated throughout both the Old and New Testaments, but it goes from black and white to technicolor as we experience our flesh-and-blood Jesus in the Gospels. Later, in Revelation, praying with holy imagination ends the Scriptures in a series of fireworks.

In the hands of God, and fueled by the Spirit, the imagination becomes one more way to experience communion with God. Since all things were created for communion, the imagination is one more doorway. In an essay titled "The Value of the Sanctified Imagination," Protestant theologian A. W. Tozer wrote, "I long to see the imagination released from its prison and given to its proper place among the Sons of the new creation."[3]

The imagination is the playground of artists and writers, engineers, city planners, and inventors. In fact, it's the birthplace of all visionary action, Thomas Edison's first moment turning on the lights, Abraham Lincoln's American landscape of freedom, and Martin Luther King Jr.'s dreams of equality. Imagination is what gave us Narnia and Aslan and your hometown botanical garden, Leonardo da Vinci's *Last Supper*, and the great feat of the twentieth century—lunar landings that could only have been dreamed up by those in love with gazing at the stars. The imagination is the canvas where creativity does its best work. It's where the Creator gives us a paintbrush and invites us to play.

C. S. Lewis wrote, "We seek an enlargement of our being. We want to be more than ourselves. . . . We want to see with other eyes, to imagine with other imaginations, to feel with other hearts, as well as with our own. . . . We demand windows."[4] Ignatian Imaginative Prayer is a cathedral of windows.

For Ignatius of Loyola, the imagination became the place where an active faith was kindled. After his knee was crushed by a cannon, Ignatius lie in bed struggling with depression, his dream of becoming a knight decimated by a single, insignificant battle. His life, he believed, was over. This ushered in a long, internal winter. Would he keep his leg? Would he end up disabled? His imagination became the place of a haunting. Until his conversion.

After his decision to give his life to follow God, Ignatius began imagining what it would be like to be God's knight and fight for His kingdom. He noticed how much joy he had after these wonderings. As he "walked onto the set" of one Gospel story after another, he noted how his desire for God grew and his hunger for holiness was compounded.[5]

Joseph Whelan, SJ, explained how further conversion occurs as a result of "falling in love with what seizes your imagination." He wrote,

Nothing is more practical than finding God,
   That is, than falling in love in a quite absolute, final way.
   What you are in love with, what seizes your imagination will af-
      fect everything.
   It will decide what will get you out of bed in the mornings,
   What you will do with your evenings,
   How you spend your weekends,
   What you read,
   Who you know,
   What breaks your heart,
And what amazes you with joy and gratitude.
Fall in love, stay in love, and it will decide everything.[6]

Just like our will, our imagination needs to be redeemed. It needs to be retrained. Worry is imagination off its leash, running toward the highway. Doubt is the malnourished imagination, having forgotten to feast on the power of God. This is why Paul invited us to "[fill our] minds and [meditate] on things true, noble, reputable, authentic, compelling, gracious" as Eugene Peterson paraphrased Philippians 4:8 in the Message.

For the malnourished imagination, Ignatian Imaginative Prayer is a feast. In order to be transformed from worry-driven to Christ following, the imagination needs to be fed the wonder of Emmanuel's presence. We need to be awed by the resurrected Christ so that the shiny, petty things of the world no longer conquer our imaginations so easily. Saint Francis de Sales explained it this way: "By means of the imagination, we confine our mind within the mystery on which we meditate, that it may not ramble to and fro, just as we shut up a bird in a cage or tie a hawk by his leash so that he may rest on the hand."[7]

Let's Practice Together

Now, let's walk onto the set of one of the Gospel stories together. Before continuing, please read the story of the woman with the issue of blood found in Luke 8:43–48.

Jesus is in a hurry, following Jairus, the synagogue leader, one of the most respected people in the village. They seem to be in an emergency. I watch the trajectory of Jesus pushing through the crowd toward me while I crouch on the gravel, one hand steadying me so I can touch Him without His knowing I touched Him. I am ritually unclean, blood dripping down my legs. Maybe if I just touch His clothes, He won't notice. He can go about His day. He won't become unclean.

It's been twelve years since I've been with my husband. Twelve years since I've been touched by a kind hand on the shoulder. Twelve years since I've been pushed to the outskirts of this village. It's been twelve years since hope slowly began draining away, one drop at a time. But here He comes, close enough to touch. As I grasp on to His hem, I feel a strength surge through my body like a potter gathering up clay, firm.

Almost immediately, He stops, stretching His arms out in the crowd, trying to make space, looking around Him—up, down, His movements almost wild. "Who touched me?" He inquires of the mass of people.

People scowl. Jesus is jam-packed in the middle of a crowd. "Who touched me?" again, He implores, searching, His eyes darting from one head to another. Slowly, I find enough strength in my legs to stand, to walk, and then to fall at His feet. There's a gasp. Everyone in this village knows who I am. Most days they give me a wide berth as I walk through the streets, scavenging for dinner at the market, trying not to meet eyes. Even the doctors try to examine me with sticks, leaving me with little dignity and less in my purse. When I stand up in front of Jesus, I hear murmurings. A few in the front row cover their noses with scarves.

Somehow here in front of Jesus, it feels safe to offer the overwhelming grief, the lost years, the devastation. As I mumble my story, Jesus slowly lowers Himself to look into my face. I'm surprised to discover eyes full of tenderness, wet with unshed tears.

I see that He knows what it feels like to be me.

With warmth in His voice, He says, "Take heart, daughter, your faith has healed you." He says it loud enough to let me know He's seen my shame and it hasn't chased Him away. He says it loud enough for the crowd to hear, loud enough to secure for me a new story in this village.

Your Story Too

Give yourself a moment to stand in these sandals, flat leather sliding over sand and gravel. Feel the warm Middle Eastern sun, the smell and sounds of an eager crowd pressed together. Then, try on her suffering, her shame, and while you're there, gather the heaviness of your own story, your own unspoken longing for healing. Maybe you need healing in your body. In a relationship. In the depression that is like a slow bleed of hope. In a desperate struggle for your soul.

Gather your courage and with this woman, reach out for Jesus.

Maybe on a normal day you're riddled with doubts.

Maybe on a normal day you don't feel worthy of His gaze.

Or maybe you like to stay self-contained, necktie in a tight knot, shoes polished, keeping the heaviness hidden, even from your own eyes.

But, friend, don't miss your opportunity; here inside this story, you get to try on the woman's courage. Give yourself permission to grasp onto Jesus's hem with raw need.

As Jesus queries the pressing crowd, "Who touched me?" stumble forward and, with the woman, tell Him your story. Uncover the shame and recognize that while it feels vulnerable in front of the crowd, somehow in Jesus's hands, it feels safe to offer the overwhelming grief, the lost years, the devastation.

Again, watch Jesus with the woman. See the tenderness in His raised brows. Tears form in the corner of His eyes, and for the first time, you feel safe enough to weep. Your story is in His hands and He's not throwing it back in your face. He sees your profound need and the stench of your shame, and He does not turn away. He moves toward you. God has seen you, and your story shifts in the light of His presence. Remember, the One who healed this precious woman is the same One who walks with you through the pain that you carry. Your Healer is there in the room with you. Maybe you've lost heart. You've been carrying this pain for so many years. Maybe you can't bring yourself to speak the words and give voice to your need, but you can grasp His hem.

Mirror Neurons and Making New Memories with God

I invite you to check in on what's happening in you right now.

Sometimes the experience of Ignatian Imaginative Prayer is so vivid, the images you saw become part of a rolodex of new memories, encounters with the living Christ. This is where we can, as Richard Foster wrote, "experience the perpetual presence of the Lord not as theological dogma but as radiant reality."[8]

Reverend Valerie McIntyre has a graduate degree in the Christian Imagination, Aquinas, and Ignatius of Loyola. Through a nine-month curriculum at Transformation Intensive, she teaches Ignatian Imaginative Prayer practices, and the people who go through this training often testify to a deepening of their connection to Jesus.[9] During an interview, Valerie told me how she has watched big truckers break down in tears, finally able to understand how loved they are by God.

Valerie also told me about mirror neurons. This is how the National Institutes of Health describes them: "Mirror neurons are a class of neuron that modulate their activity both when an individual executes a specific motor act and when they observe the same or similar act performed by another individual."[10]

If that just sounded like a bunch of scientific jargon, listen to this story. In 1992, scientists who were studying monkeys in Parma, Italy, discovered that the same brain cells fired when a monkey was watching another monkey eating a banana as if he himself were experiencing the peeling and action of taking a bite.[11]

This is mirror neurons in action. When we see someone experience something, our brain responds as if we are experiencing it too. Mirror neurons cause our mouths to water as we watch the *Great British Baking Show*. Through her work, Valerie has made connections between mirror neurons and Ignatian Imaginative Prayer. Let's imagine the following and get our own mirror neurons firing.

First, as we watch Jesus interact with people in the Gospels, we begin to imagine what it would be like to experience His walking in our present reality. For instance, perhaps you walk into the Gospel story of Jesus blessing the children. You watch Jesus blessing another child as you sit under a tree in the distance, His tenderness in full display. As you watch, you begin to notice His full attention on that other child's face. He leans down to their level and looks into their eyes. You imagine Him glancing toward the mother with a smile on His face, learning this other child's name. You see Him cupping the child's chin. As you watch, you begin to "put on" the gift of what it would be like to be with this Jesus.

As we gaze on Jesus gazing on another, we begin to picture that the love of God has wide enough arms for us. We get to know Jesus's personality. We may have been taught about Jesus by adults who were not attentive, who were always looking at a to-do list or glancing over our heads at someone "more important." But when we experience Jesus present with these children, all that shifts. Our view of a disengaged God who is always focused on something "more important" is challenged. We begin to desire a relationship with Him, to have His tender gaze resting on us. We follow Him around in the Gospels and wonder what it would be like to follow *this* Jesus in every aspect of our lives.

Second, as we watch Jesus, we move into the stage of imitation. In Ephesians 5:1–2, Paul invites us to "be *imitators* of God, *as beloved children*. And walk in love, as Christ loved us" (ESV, emphasis added).

We watch Emmanuel's habits, slipping away into prayer, inviting disciples into His most vulnerable moments, giving attention to "the least of these." Just like a toddler with a play kitchen mirrors their mother as she makes dinner, a child-size wooden spoon in a child-size bowl, we learn by watching. We carefully study and become imitators, sent out into the highways and byways, looking for opportunities to invite people to come to His table.

But third, as we enter the story, mirror neurons at work, sometimes we expect cozy familiarity and, instead, are confronted by His otherness. We are shocked by His beauty, shocked by His unveiled power, shocked that He is outside of time and space. We fall flat on our faces in worship. We see this when we take a hike with Jesus, Peter, James, and John, climbing what we know as the Mount of Transfiguration. We behold Him, the One enthroned—the Alpha and Omega. Wisdom enfleshed. We realize we have only the most elementary idea of who walks beside us on the trail. We sit, stunned and silent until He touches us and tells us it's time to go home, and then, we carry awe inside us like a seed.

Attachment and Imaginative Prayer

In Ignatian Imaginative Prayer we learn to ground our nervous systems to the presence of Jesus. When we encounter Him, we discover the Alpha and Omega walking on the waves of our life and know we are not alone. Sure, the circumstances have not shifted. The wind buffets. The whitecaps break, but Emmanuel, the Prince of Peace, is present. As we cry out "Lord, save me," our Rescuer is quick to respond. By experiencing the presence of our Emmanuel through the holy imagination, we receive an earned, secure attachment.

Remember how I said we are transformed in repetition and lingering? We can close our eyes and nightly visit the story of Jesus blessing the children, feeling His warm hand on our head, hearing His blessing, His calling our name. Daily, we can listen to His "Peace be still" as the hurricane causing havoc in our lives obeys His voice. We can sit and gape at our Emmanuel's last breaths and watch the lengths He was willing to go to take care of our sin and keep us near Him for all eternity. Each time we find ourselves grieving, we can sit in front of the tomb on that early Easter morning and feel the earthquake and watch the stone being rolled away, knowing He has conquered death's finality.

We can visit and keep visiting while the Word mends us, and the more time we spend in His presence, the less we want to leave. We determine to follow Him everywhere.

––––––––

Access videos where I lead you through various Ignatian Imaginative Prayer exercises, including the woman with the issue of blood at summerjoygross.com/the-emmanuel-promise.

19

Lament

Welcomed as We Are

Definition: Lament is a form of prayer in which the details of our sorrow and the heaviness of our emotions are voiced before our God, who has an infinite capacity to carry them. Lament is uncensored, sometimes written, sometimes spoken with a safe person.

Attachment Principle: Lament is an invitation to experience attunement with God, who "tunes in" to the suffering of His children. Just like for an infant, crying out is the key to our bond with God. Our every cry becomes a bid for attachment. If we try to manage on our own, we miss the opportunity for care. Crying out is our job.

Scripture: "The hearts of the people cry out to the Lord. . . . Let your tears flow like a river day and night; . . . Arise, cry out in the night; . . . pour out your heart like water in the presence of the Lord" (Lam. 2:18–19).
"You have kept count of my tossings; put my tears in your bottle. Are they not in your book?" (Ps. 56:8 ESV).

How to Lament

Identify a grief, anger, place of despair, or another sorrow.
Address God.

Write down the details of this part of your story. Be honest. Include how each moment in your story felt and what it has cost you emotionally, physically, spiritually, and relationally. Stay present to your emotions as you write.

Let the words flow uncensored. Don't hold back, cross out, or worry about punctuation and grammar or "doing it right."

End by turning back to God, either recounting His faithfulness, writing what you know of His character, or asking Him to help you identify a place of hope in your story.

Find a safe person, spiritual director, pastor, or therapist to be an empathetic witness and read it to them in a sacred space.

Immanuel Journaling

In Immanuel Journaling, we look at our experience from Jesus's viewpoint and listen to His attuning presence.[1] We begin by writing an emotionally poignant gratitude and then listening to how our Abba feels about our sharing this gratitude. Tell Him why you're thankful for that specific memory.

1. I see you: Write from God's perspective how He sees you right now, including your physical sensations. *"I can see you at your desk. Your breathing is shallow. Your shoulders are tight."*
2. I hear you: Write from God's perspective what you are saying to yourself.
3. I know how big this is for your story: Write how God sees your dreams, blessings, upsets, or troubles.
4. I am glad to be with you and treat your weaknesses tenderly: Write how God desires to participate in your life.
5. I can do something about what you're going through: Ask God what resources He has for you at this time.

Each Cry, a Bid for Attachment

After thirty-two hours of labor, Caedmon was placed in my arms, unearthly quiet, his blue-grey eyes wide open and blinking at me. It was my mother-in-law, who had spent sixteen years on a maternity ward, who mentioned his lips looked slightly blue. In this case, silence was not a good sign. Cries are the only language an infant knows. Cries are crucial.

At Mom's suggestion, Caedmon was rushed off to a nearby table, where his nose and mouth were cleaned out, body rubbed, oxygen applied. My mother-in-law had been my doula. She drove to the hospital from Ohio. After hours of labor, she must have been exhausted as well. I'm grateful she wasn't lulled by the quiet like the rest of us were.

Silence, of course, is not always a sign of contentment; sometimes it's a sign of distress. Sometimes silence means a need has been strangled. For the next three years, Caedmon's cry would be the preamble to a need being met and, ultimately, for attachment being created. Every time a caregiver calibrates their response to meet their infant's need, they are attuning. They hear the cry and observe, doing their best to respond appropriately.

Think about the job of a piano tuner. They take time plinking on the piano, tightening or loosening the strings, making sure the tone resonates perfectly. Attunement means dialing into a need, making thoughtful assessment, and giving a thoughtful response. Suffice it to say, without attunement, attachment is not a possibility.

Months before Caedmon was born, I found a paperback of *Secrets of the Baby Whisperer* at a brightly lit Barnes & Noble forty-five minutes' drive up Lake Michigan. "Sleep through the night in six weeks," the cover said. Sold! It came home tucked in my leather bag.

Inside the appendix was a graph, an infant cry decoder. I was fascinated. Aren't all cries the same? The author said no. You can learn the language of your baby's cry by looking at their body language. If your baby is tired, they'll turn their head to the side, looking away. Stomachache? They'll pull their legs into their stomach when they're crying. Hungry? They'll root around. Listen and watch before you act, the author advised. At the core of attachment is knowing that if we cry out, our caregiver will come running.

One observer of Russian and Romanian Cold War orphanages said the orphanages were silent, bizarrely silent. As he walked through the hallways, he saw rows of babies in cribs, laying on their backs. All was well, or was it? These babies had lost the belief that their cries would be answered. They had succumbed to despair. They did not believe anyone was coming so they had ceased sharing their need. Their mental and physical health would suffer greatly for their learned silence.[2]

Crying out is also the key to our attachment bond with God. Our every cry becomes a bid for attachment. If we try to manage on our own, we miss the opportunity for our own attachment with God.

Think of husbands and wives who whisper their concerns to each other at the end of the day, their heads leaning together as they sit on the couch, holding each other's stories. Andrew and I often do this over tacos at Silver Queen. We sit in the corner over a single margarita and street corn, and as our stories are kindly held, our pain gets lighter. We have an empathetic witness, someone who joins us in our pain. Pain is lessoned as we look into each other's eyes.[3]

David shows us the way in the Psalms. He was called "a man after God's own heart," not because he didn't sin. His sins are well known. But on the steep hills of Bethlehem, while minding sheep, David gave his emotions a voice. Nothing was off-limits in this constant conversation. He brought guilt and gladness, anger, depression, fear, and jealousy to the Lord. As David felt safe enough to invite the Lord into the tender places of his heart, he received the attachment that gave him the courage to kill giants.

After our cries are met by our caregiver, we begin to trust. We internalize the belief that we are not alone and there is someone who will care the next time we cry out. This is how attachment is formed. In Psalm 56:8, we receive a clear sign that our cry is welcomed by

God: "You have kept count of my tossings; put my tears in your bottle. Are they not in your book?" (ESV). He is paying attention, tuning in, collecting our pain, even when we're not aware. He even journals our tears, catching the story of the ones we wipe away.

When we grieve the death of a loved one and reach out to God, the waves of grief come like contractions. As we sense God turned toward us, we steady ourselves in a strange slow dance of sadness, or we crumble to the ground and find that He was there already. Looking into our eyes. Holding our hand through the journey.

He Meets Us in Our Suffering

Our most recent move was to a city where I could not get a job as a priest. I had been a priest for over eleven years already, ten as an assistant in a parish. For months I woke up around dawn with my heart racing and the need to move. I'd steer our minivan to the nearby church, entering into a dark, silent sanctuary, taking off my shoes, and stepping onto the plush, red carpet with my bare feet. As I passed the baptismal font, I marked the cross on my forehead with the cool water. Then I laid face down in front of the altar, arms out, cruciform. I was laying down my grief before God. It was the only cry I could muster. There was a strange relief, embodying grief. The floor held me up. It did not give way. As I turned my head to the right, I sensed Jesus there beside me, fingertip to fingertip. He was looking into my eyes. "I do this all the time," I sensed Him say. He was present, a witness to my grief. In His eyes, I began to trust my story would not be wasted. Sometimes our grief needs more than words; it needs to be embodied.

The Keys to Lament

First, listen for the lament.

You know you need to lament when grief stays, guilt pricks, resentment builds, unmet longings surprise you as tears sting, jealousy closes the door to gratefulness, fear from the past starts shutting the doors of your future, you desire to isolate because *how could they understand* the heaviness you're living with. You fear oversharing will scare them away.

Also, and this is essential, your lament doesn't have a shelf life. God doesn't have a rule of one and done. Each repeated lament is treasured. Remember, the cross reminds us that God has unlimited capacity to hold your pain. Bring it all to His loving arms.

Second, write a lament that is uncensored. The more detailed the lament, the better. The more emotionally raw, the greater the healing. Write down not just the specifics but also the corresponding feelings that arise. If this is hard to do, get out a feeling wheel. Then, ask yourself, What was the true cost of this pain—emotionally, physically, spiritually, even relationally?

Third—and please, don't skimp on this step—let your lament be held. We need an embodied witness for our tears, someone to hold the hard and holy. Healing is deepened as pain rises and is heard by an empathetic listener, a spiritual director, a pastor, a therapist, or a wise and safe friend. Remember, even Jesus desired companions in the garden of Gethsemane. He knew that as our pain is witnessed by safe, loving people, it is reduced.

We are grateful for Jesus's obedience in going to the cross, but we forget, before our Emmanuel surrendered to Golgotha, He wept. He lamented. He allowed His fear to find a voice. He begged for relief, for a different way. He cried out to be heard, and His wrestling was so emotionally taxing, He sweat drops of blood. And then, after His weeping, He was attended to by angels, bringing the comfort of His Father. After the lament and the Father's attunement, He was able to walk the Via Dolorosa.

Attachment love developed through attunement gives us the resilience to risk the courage of obedience.

Still trying to get your mind around this practice? By now, you know that I'll lead you through step-by-step. At summerjoy gross.com/the-emmanuel-promise, you can find a free workbook leading you through three different kinds of laments. Just push play.

Conclusion

Stewarding the Presence

We abide, attaching to God through all of the practices you've just read about. Again, the Spirit will lead you to others. He is your ardent companion on the journey.

- We become aware and awake to the presence of Emmanuel, available for attachment, with practices like watching a flickering candle, using a prayer posture, or fingering a tangible object like a clinging cross.
- We experience the gentle correction of Divine Love and His turning toward us, inviting us to experience repentance as an invitation to reattach.
- We slow down the Word through Lectio Divina, allowing it to do its deep work in us, binding us to our Abba, while we create enough space to listen relationally in the silence.
- We encounter and dwell in Love with the simple practice of the 3 R's: Rest, Receive, and Respond.
- We quiet our nervous systems in the presence of Emmanuel with breath prayer, resting as a child leaning against the chest and regulating to the heartbeat of a loving caregiver.
- We create intentional silence, cocooning with God, scheduling quality time together to recognize where our disordered

attachments lie and start looking toward our Perfect Caregiver.

- We experience God's attunement through lament or Immanuel Journaling, feeling safe, seen, soothed, and secure through suffering.
- We walk into the Word in an encounter through holy imagination by dwelling with the Emmanuel in the Gospels through Ignatian Imaginative Prayer.

As we find sanctuary in His heart, our God-with-us becomes uninhibited God-in-us. But God-with-us is not for us alone; God-with-us is a multiplier because Love always multiplies.

Here's the thing. Our attachment wound not only inhibits us from experiencing security and safety in *our* everyday lives, it dams up the life of Christ in us, hindering us from loving well. We become reactionary in our relationships, harming and being harmed. As we receive the attachment of our Emmanuel, we are able to ride the waves of conflict and rejection, buoyed by the God who holds our identity firm. We are able to stay anchored in the midst of suffering.

Our attachment wound also restricts other abilities. To create courageously. To invite others to the feast. And to risk obedience out of trust.

Courage is developed through a secure attachment with God. We can choose the vulnerability of saying yes to the way God invites us to naturally steward the presence of God in our everyday life. "My soul doth magnify the Lord" is the response of a life fueled by attachment love (Luke 1:46 KJV). Like Mary, we become bearers of Emmanuel.

The Christmas of 2004, I was nine months pregnant with Caedmon, a year into being ordained. As I preached in tandem with my husband, my body was being stretched like Mary's. We processed down the aisle on Advent Sundays, wearing purple stoles, my own making a giant detour around my belly. We sang "O Come, O Come, Emmanuel" and Caedmon's tiny back pressed into my ribs in utero, making it hard to sing, to get enough air. Mary's story and my story became inextricably linked.

I was fascinated. She was the first bearer of the Story, the Word Himself. A young girl had said yes to bear God inside her skin. Just now as I write this, I wonder if she was handpicked because she "treasured all these things" already. She was a noticer, a wonderer, a treasurer.[1] She turned aside to gaze at every flaming bush, gathering the glimmers to narrate the story later. She herself became a human container for the flame, the Holy of Holies stretching her from within.

The Servant as Birthgiver

In the icon Our Lady of the Sign, Jesus is within Mary, a miniature, fully formed man, hand raised in blessing. Her womb is cut in half like a watermelon, and we have a circular window into it. We witness the presence of God she's carrying into the world. She was the first Christian, the first to say yes to God, responding "may it be to me according to your word." As poet Denise Levertov penned, "Consent illumined her."[2] She did not yet know how much she would be stretched by the pain of her yes, stretched by surrender.

After Gabriel left, Mary must have known that her God-filled adventure would look different from other girls' tidy stories. As she watched her son struggle for breath on the cross, did she wonder if her surrender was being snuffed out, whether it had all been worth it? Our yes sometimes leads to an outcome that looks nothing like the vision we thought we conceived. Can we say a daily yes to carrying God's life within us even if it ends up looking nothing like we first envisioned?

Intercessor

As Mary walked into every room, she carried God enfleshed within her flesh, the life of Christ for the world. Inside her body was the

Savior, the Rescuer, the One who sang stars into being. The Word who never stopped speaking. The Healer, Redeemer, Wave-stiller, and the One over whom death has no power. She walked into the room and so did Life Himself.

On Christmas Eve, I stood behind the altar. My large belly touched the table. "Our Father," Andrew and I began, and a whole chorus of folks dressed in reds and greens and golds joined us. "Who art in heaven. Hallowed be Thy name. Thy kingdom come. Thy will be done. On earth as it is in heaven." I placed my palms on the brocade white tablecloth.

Your kingdom come. Here.

Just like Mary, when we stay attached, aware of the presence of God in our bodies, we consciously walk the Emmanuel into every room. We proclaim, "Your kingdom come, here." We plant the presence of Emmanuel in the room as a flag, inviting the work of God to spread through every person, healing, redeeming, resurrecting. His promise of presence becomes our privilege.

Remember, nestled within you is the Spirit of Emmanuel, a fire of justice, a flame of love, the Christ life Himself. The kingdom of God is within. Emmanuel desires to transform us from the inside out. He also desires to transform our world through us.

When we practice the presence of God as we walk down the sidewalks of our neighborhoods, we pray, *Your Kingdom come. Your will be done. Here.* We walk into a coffeehouse and ask the question, Lord, how would You like me to care for Your beloveds here?

This "bearing the presence" requires a new pace, a pace conducive to listening to the voice of Love. We practice the presence of God and the presence of the one in front of us simultaneously, open to His heart for them. As we curl up our legs on the couch and practice the presence of the image of God in the one across from us, sipping coffee and holding their story, our attention becomes the pregnant moment in which they can experience God's kindness through our eyes. Political activist Simone Weil said "attention is the rarest and purest form of generosity."[3]

Monday Morning Practical: Compassion

Try it out. Go to a busy Starbucks at seven in the morning, and as people rush in and out, ask the Emmanuel to give you eyes to see His love for this one unique expression of His creativity or to gift you with a picture of their pain. Practice the presence of God with this person standing on the threshold of their day, one glorious being, broken and beautiful, at a time. Ask and then pray His heart for them. Look around at the faces of those lost in the glow of their screens and ask the Emmanuel to flood you with His first majestic idea of their creation, what He meant when He carefully crafted *them*! Become "easily delighted" with created art in human form. Fall in love a thousand times over. Then, attached and courageous enough to risk, make yourself available to the Emmanuel's mission: to speak good news to the poor, rescue captives, bind up broken hearts, comfort mourners. To draw all people into attachment love with their Emmanuel, the One who longs to fill every empty heart.

Then go to the homeless shelter, to the prison, to the boutique, to the boat docks. Walk the light of Christ into the corners of the world.

Pray God would make every ordinary location a sanctuary of His presence.

Whenever we are in the presence of another human soul, we are standing on holy ground. God knew them first, watched as they grew and somersaulted in the womb. He celebrated with the other persons of the Trinity when they entered the delivery room. His unique design on their soul was etched art. They are loved ecstatically even as they, too, need His attachment love.

Loving Out of a Secure Attachment

By this time in the book, Dear One, I hope you've pushed the heaviness of shame right off your lap and begun to view your attachment story with more compassion. I hope you've started to catch even the tiniest glimpse of what a secure attachment could feel like. As one beautiful Presence Project member said, "As I become more attached to God, I feel quiet on the inside."

You are His beloved, adopted through blood and baptism, His chosen. Every time you soak in the presence of God using a Lectio Divina, an Ignatian Imaginative Prayer, or one of the other practices, you are carving out time to receive God's promised attachment. You are doing the hard work of building new neural pathways, one practice at a time.

Now, as you receive a secure attachment, God's generous love allows you to be a beginner, loving through awkward fits and starts. Hidden in the heart of your Beloved, you have the courage to say yes to imperfection, yes to small, yes to creativity for the sake of joy, not an ego-driven destiny.

You are still fragile and vulnerable and imperfect and awkward, but recognizing your imperfections doesn't send you into isolation anymore. As you become secure in love, you can be awkward *and* generous. You can be confused and not have all the answers *and* stay present. You can be curious with your sinful tendencies, ask for forgiveness, *and* live in God's grace.

You will see people, really see them, not for what your ego can get but with a detached, yet substantial love. You'll find you're more generous with your heart but careful with your time.

As you have learned to rest in the refuge of God's heart, your ego is starting to be quieted. Like an infant trying to get its needs met, your ego has been quite demanding up until now. You needed an audience, a title, a constant IV drip of validation. Now you are beginning to recognize you don't have to jump up and down and raise your voice, fearful there won't be love enough, care enough, dignity enough. You may even find yourself surprised at a lack of motivation. The old desires to compete and cajole just don't seem to have the oomph.

This is a journey, much like a labyrinth, where you catch a view of the center and then turn a corner and struggle to believe you're headed in the right direction. You may get caught up once again in a cycle of starving and striving, but in the back of your mind, you always know the way home:

1. Come awake to His promised presence with you right here.
2. Lament and receive His attunement and comfort.
3. Linger in love.

Year after year, the path gets more familiar, but it always begins with practicing your Emmanuel's presence. But don't worry, I don't expect you've arrived. Yes, you've begun to "taste and see that God is good," and these encounters with your Emmanuel are still resonating. But this is just the beginning.

You may want to keep this Teilhard de Chardin poem close for a while:

> Above all, trust in the slow work of God.
> We are quite naturally impatient in everything to reach the
>   end without delay.
> We should like to skip the intermediate stages.
> We are impatient of being on the way to something
> unknown, something new.
>
> And yet it is the law of all progress
> that it is made by passing through some stages of
>   instability—
> and that it may take a very long time.
>
> And so I think it is with you . . .
>
> Only God could say what this new spirit
> gradually forming within you will be.
> Give Our Lord the benefit of believing
> that his hand is leading you,
> and accept the anxiety of feeling yourself
> in suspense and incomplete.[4]

This is a pilgrimage, Dear One, and you have an ardent Companion, a determined Healer, and an Abba who is always looking for ways to pull you close. Let this journey be one in which, instead of striving, you learn to fall backwards into His waiting arms over and over again. Your Emmanuel has promised to always be waiting.

Keep lingering.

He is leading.

You are becoming.

Trust in the slow work of God.

Today you are invited to live braided into the open arms of the Trinity.

———

You're at the finish line, but remember, these practices are made to be done in repetition over a lifetime. Listen to the Spirit's promptings. You're not trying to become an expert; you're learning to become the beloved. At summerjoygross.com/the-emmanuel-promise, you'll find a Lectio Divina on Jesus reminding us our identity is that we are called to be light; there is also one on Ephesians 2:10.

Acknowledgments

As a writer, I've always seen myself as the voice of a community. Ideas are developed in community. People are formed in community. This book is the same.

The ideas in this book and the person I've become as I've drawn near to Jesus have been formed with the folks at Healing Care Ministries. Dr. Terry Wardle and Dr. Anne Halley, you have been cultivating these ideas long before me. Your work has been the crucible for my healing, my formation in spiritual direction, the foundation of the Presence Project, and, of course, this book. I hope you see this book as part of your legacy. Also a big thank-you to Dr. Neal Siler, Robert Woodcock, and Sarah Herring for how you've shaped my perspective on spiritual direction.

Thank you to the Presence Project community. Wow. Your stories have been woven through every sentence, explicit or not. You have amazed me as I've gotten to witness you grow closer to Jesus. I am an extrovert, and I could not have done such intense inner work without you, especially Alison Bradley, Sue Fulmore, Lori Whitaker, Jan Bennett, Stacy Jessel, and Jean Gassett. It's been a privilege to serve the Presence Project folks with you.

Thank you to the small groups in South Haven, Michigan; Ambridge, Pennsylvania; and Loganville, Georgia—for being willing to engage this work with me in the flesh. God showed up time and time again, and I couldn't help but take off my shoes and worship.

Thank you to Rose-Marie Tasker Edwards and the many others who prayed this work into being. I'm just so grateful for the quiet, powerful work you do.

I also write my best words in community. Thank you, Lane Mathis Arnold, for being half writing coach, half spiritual director every Monday morning. Thank you to my first coach, Jenni Bartling, for setting off this spark. Thank you also to Kara Yuza, my brilliant admin assistant. You keep the Presence Project moving steadily through all my creative deep dives.

Thank you, Nicole Mazzarella, for meeting me at one airport or another for writing retreats. Working in silence with you during the day and then sharing long, beautiful meals each night was the perfect formula for this creative work. Thank you also for using your masterly professor mind to engage unwieldy chapters.

Thank you to the Sunrise Sisters who met me at the cottage and informed this work through their abundant inner lives, especially Terrie Caisley, who held the hard and holy stories of my family and led me into Jesus's presence.

Thank you to the writers who walked with me through the awkward steps of the publishing journey, as well as those at Hope*writers and in my mastermind—Jodi Grubbs, Kris Camealy, Maeve Gerboth, Julianne Clayton, and Bette Dickinson. Thank you also to K. J. Ramsey, who is the patron saint of our large, amorphous writing community.

Thank you to Ben and Lauren Brown who were my Old Testament and Hebrew language advisors. Your enthusiasm for Scripture is a joy.

Thank you to my agent, Mary DeMuth, who expertly shepherds me and all her folks through the labyrinth of the publishing industry by going before us and showing us the way.

To my editor at Baker Publishing Group, Stephanie Duncan Smith, who brought clarity out of my messy sketch and helped me frame this book. Thank you to my coeditor, Andy Rogers. This is a much better book because you were liberal with your red pen. Thank you also to Robin Turici for your attention to detail and to everyone else at Baker. You are brilliant book midwives.

I'm also deeply thankful for the work of Brennan Manning, Kallistos Ware, Leanne Payne, C. S. Lewis, and Henri Nouwen. Their theology has informed my life for the last twenty-plus years. Thank you also to Dr. Curt Thompson whose generous book *Anatomy of the Soul* has undergirded much of this conversation about healing attachment wounds and spiritual formation. My copy is worn and dog-eared, attesting to how many times I've read the chapters, highlighter in hand.

Mom and Dad, I had no idea how healing it would be to write this book. Thank you for being so gracious to let me explore my story on the page. Mom, thank you for being a creative cothinker. Thank you, Dad, for the many vacation days you sat editing with me at the wooden table and then taking me sailing afterwards. Thank you both for how well you love our family. I'm so extremely grateful.

Thank you to my three siblings and their spouses who encouraged me to keep putting pen to paper and cared for my children this July so I could finish this work.

Thank you to my husband, Andrew, who calls himself my pit crew, sears a perfect rib eye, dances with me in the kitchen, and shows me the kindness of Jesus in a thousand different ways. Thank you to my three beautiful kids, Caedmon, Maddie Pearl, and Xavier. May you always know that you are "marked as Christ's own forever."

Notes

Introduction

1. Beatriz Luna, "Development of Frontal GABA and Glutamate Supports Excitation/Inhibition Balance from Adolescence into Adulthood," *Progress in Neurobiology* (2022), accessed June 22, 2023, https://neurosciencenews.com/neuroplasticity-teen-brain-21807/.

2. Perry S. Nelson, Jane M. Simoni, and Howard S. Adelman, "Mobility and School Functioning in the Early Grades," *The Journal of Educational Research* 89, no. 6 (1996), https://doi.org/http://doi.org/10.1080/00220671.1996.9941340.

3. Daniel J. Siegel, *Mindsight: The New Science of Personal Transformation* (New York: Bantam Books, 2010), 135.

4. "Developmental Sciences at UMass Boston," YouTube video, posted by UMass Boston, March 10, 2010, https://youtu.be/vmE3NfB_HhE.

5. This is why parental phone use can be so destructive. For a child, it is often experienced as Still Face.

6. This illustration reflects an experiential teaching in the curriculum for Healing Care Groups by Terry Wardle, which I highly recommend.

7. Much of the work of this book is built upon the foundation Dr. Anne Halley laid during this conference, including the books she suggested. She's brilliant. If you ever have a chance to learn from her, you're going to want to take that opportunity.

8. *Letters to Malcolm* by CS Lewis © copyright 1963, 1964 CS Lewis Pte Ltd. Extract used with permission.

9. Brother Lawrence, *The Practice of the Presence of God: Brother Lawrence of the Resurrection* (New York: Crown Publishing Group, 1977), 49.

10. Brother Lawrence, *Practice of the Presence of God*, 28.

11. The Presence Project is a group working to discover how to overcome anxiety through ancient contemplative practices and the corroboration of neuroscience. With Lectio Divina videos, spiritual direction groups, and monthly retreats led by me, it's a great place to start if you're interested in finding others on this journey.

Chapter 1 Your First Attachment Stories

1. Allan N. Schore, "Attachment and the Regulation of the Right Brain," *Attachment & Human Development* 2, no. 1 (2000): 10, https://www.allanschore.com/pdf/SchoreAttachHumDev.pdf.

2. This curriculum is brilliant. I call it Discipleship 901. I've seen so many people get free. How do you discover what has you bound? How do you receive the healing of Jesus in your deepest wounds? Don't do it alone. It's in community that God does His best work. Find a group near you or online at https://www.healingcare.org/healing-care-group-curriculum.

3. I. Bretherton, "The Origins of Attachment Theory: John Bowlby and Mary Ainsworth," *Developmental Psychology* 28, no. 5 (1992): 759–75, https://doi.org/10.1037/0012-1649.28.5.759; Sue Johnson, *Hold Me Tight: Seven Conversations for a Lifetime of Love* (New York: Little, Brown Spark, 2008), Introduction; "John Bowlby," Wikipedia, accessed March 13, 2023, https://en.wikipedia.org/w/index.php?title=John_Bowlby&oldid=1154643004.

4. Curt Thompson, *Anatomy of the Soul: Surprising Connections Between Neuroscience and Spiritual Practices That Can Transform Your Life and Relationships* (Carol Stream, IL: Tyndale, 2010), 117.

5. Schore, "Attachment and the Regulation of the Right Brain."

6. Thompson, *Anatomy of the Soul*, 116.

7. I will keep touching on the need for community throughout the book, though the main focus of *The Emmanuel Promise* is on attachment practices, which enable us to receive attachment from God. The truth is that we desperately need both, for healing and for simply being human.

8. Jeffrey Olrick and Amy Elizabeth Olrick, *The 6 Needs of Every Child: Empowering Parents and Kids Through the Science of Connection* (Grand Rapids: Zondervan, 2020), 64–68.

Chapter 2 Insecure Anxious Attachment

1. Jock Gordon, *Anxious Attachment Style Workbook* (The Attachment Project, 2021).

2. Mary D. Salter Ainsworth and Silvia M. Bell, "Attachment, Exploration, and Separation: Illustrated by the Behavior of One-Year-Olds in a Strange Situation," *Child Development* 41, no. 1 (March 1970): 49–67, https://doi.org/10.2307/1127388; Amir Levine and Rachel Heller, *Attached: The New Science of Adult Attachment and How It Can Help You Find—and Keep—Love* (London: Penguin Publishing Group, 2012), 160–62; Thompson, *Anatomy of the Soul*, 127–28.

3. Again, this material is based in Healing Care Group material and Dr. Anne Halley's list of Core Longing Needs. You can find more information at https://www.healingcare.org/healing-care-group-curriculum.

4. Schore, "Attachment and the Regulation of the Right Brain."

5. This list was created by Dr. Anne Haley to understand our most basic human needs and is explained in Healing Care Ministries' Healing Care Group Curriculum.

6. This came from a family conversation around people we knew who were still stuck in food scarcity after the Great Depression and how that filtered into their children's lives.

7. This story can be found in John 4:1–30.

8. *The Problem of Pain* by CS Lewis © copyright 1940 CS Lewis Pte Ltd. Extract used with permission.

Chapter 3 Insecure Avoidant Attachment

1. Levine and Heller, *Attached*, 159–60; K. Bartholomew and L. M. Horowitz, "Attachment Styles among Young Adults: A Test of a Four-Category Model," *Journal of Personality and Social Psychology* 61, no. 2 (1991): 226, https://doi.org/10.1037//0022 -3514.61.2.226; K. A. Brennan and P. R. Shaver, "Dimensions of Adult Attachment, Affect Regulation, and Romantic Relationship Functioning," *Personality and Social Psychology Bulletin* 21, no. 3 (1995): 267–83, https://doi.org/10.1177/0146167295213008; G. Boccato and D. Capozza, "Attachment Styles and Social Groups: Review of a Decade," *TPM–Testing, Psychometrics, Methodology in Applied Psychology* 18 (2011): 19–30, https://psycnet.apa.org/record/2011-08144-002; S. B. Richman, C. N. DeWall, and M. N. Wolff, "Avoiding Affection, Avoiding Altruism: Why Is Avoidant Attachment Related to Less Helping?," *Personality and Individual Differences* 76 (2015): 193–97, https://doi.org/10.1016/j.paid.2014.12.018.

2. Thomas Merton, *No Man Is an Island* (San Diego: Harcourt Brace, 2002).

3. Thomas Merton, *The Seven Storey Mountain* (San Diego: Harcourt Brace, 1999), 63.

4. Romans 12:2: "Do not conform to the pattern of this world, but be transformed by the renewing of your mind. Then you will be able to test and approve what God's will is—his good, pleasing and perfect will."

Chapter 4 Insecure Disorganized Attachment

1. Mark T. Greenberg, Dante Cicchetti, and E. Mark Cummings, eds., *Attachment in the Preschool Years: Theory, Research, and Intervention* (Chicago: University of Chicago Press, 1990), 121–25; M. D. S. Ainsworth, M. C. Blehar, E. Waters, and S. N. Wall, "Patterns of Attachment: A Psychological Study of the Strange Situation," *Taylor & Francis* (1978), https://psycnet.apa.org/record/1980-50809-000.

2. Samantha Reisz, Robbie Duschinsky, and Daniel J. Siegel, "Disorganized Attachment and Defense: Exploring John Bowlby's Unpublished Reflections," *Attachment & Human Development* 20, no. 2 (2018): 107–34, https://doi.org/10.1080/14616734.2017 .1380055.

3. Jock Gordon, *Disorganised Attachment Style* Workbook (The Attachment Project, 2021).

4. Patricia Long, *Great to Grace: True Stories for Those in Need to Those Who Lead Through His Amazing Grace* (self-published, 2019), 7–8.

5. A great place to start would be the Come Away with Me retreat by Healing Care Ministries, a Healing Care Group, or a personal retreat at the Healing Care Center in Ashland, Ohio. The leaders are highly trained and can even lead a Healing Care Group online.

Chapter 5 Becoming Securely Attached

1. Olrick and Olrick, *6 Needs of Every Child*, 13.

2. Olrick and Olrick, *6 Needs of Every Child*, 37.

3. See Romans 8:34; Hebrews 7:25; and 1 John 2:1.

Chapter 6 Dark Night of the Soul

1. See Genesis 32:22–32 and 28:10–22.

2. The term "Dark Night of the Soul" came out of this collection of poems by St. John of the Cross: *Dark Night of the Soul by St. John of the Cross*, trans. David Lewis (London: Thomas Baker, 1908).

3. *Letter to Mary Margaret McCaslin* by CS Lewis © copyright CS Lewis Pte Ltd. Extract used with permission.

4. Miguel de Unamuno and Salvador de Madariaga, *The Tragic Sense of Life in Men and in Peoples* (London: Macmillan, 1921), 193.

5. In John 11:21, Martha told Jesus, "If you had been here, my brother would not have died."

Chapter 7 A Doorway for Connection

1. This was the simple statement of faith author Leanne Payne invited people to pray as they were establishing the truth of God's presence.

2. Henry Cloud, *Changes That Heal: How to Understand Your Past to Ensure a Healthier Future* (Grand Rapids: Zondervan, 1996), 52–53.

3. Cloud, *Changes That Heal*, 52–53.

4. Make sure you take precautions with the candle, like blowing out the flame when you go out of the house or go to sleep.

Chapter 9 Saint Patrick Shows the Way

1. Saint Patrick, *My Name Is Patrick: St Patrick's Confessio*, trans. Padraig McCarthy (Dublin, Ireland: Royal Irish Academy, 2011), 5–6.

2. You can read a free, short, and fascinating translation here: https://files.roman roadsstatic.com/uploads/2015/06/StPatrickConfession-V2-0.pdf.

3. Leanne Payne, *Heaven's Calling: A Memoir of One Soul's Steep Ascent* (Grand Rapids: Baker Books, 2008).

4. Oswald Chambers, *My Utmost for His Highest: Classic Language Edition (A Daily Devotional with 366 Bible-Based Readings)* (Grand Rapids: Our Daily Bread Publishing, 2011), July 16.

5. Cloud, *Changes That Heal*, 63–64.

Chapter 10 Holy in the Mundane

1. Jonathan Blair, "To Open the Doors of Communication, Go through the Window," Blair Psychology, January 24, 2021, https://www.drjblair.com/blog/2021/1/24 /to-open-the-doors-of-communication-go-through-the-window.

2. Denise Levertov, *The Stream & the Sapphire: Selected Poems on Religious Themes* (London, UK: New Directions, 1997), 15.

3. This is a common paraphrase of Walt Whitman from "Once I Pass'd through a Populous City," in *Leaves of Grass*, first ed. (1855) (New York: Penguin Publishing Group, 1961), lines 5–6, 94.

4. Psalm 78:19, "They spoke against God; they said, 'Can God really spread a table in the wilderness?'"

5. Ten minutes of stillness is a part of the healing of the brain that is high in the intuitive *N* on the Myers-Briggs Type Indicator. The senses begin to help an overly intuitive mind quiet and rest in the present moment.

6. Daniel Siegel, *Aware: The Science and Practice of Presence* (New York: Tarcher-Perigee, 2018), 49.

7. E. James Wilder et al., *Joy Starts Here: The Transformation Zone* (n.p.: Shepherd's House, Incorporated, 2014).

8. Derek Walcott, "Love After Love," *Collected Poems, 1948–1984* (London: Farrar, Straus and Giroux, 1986), 384.

9. If you don't have a church or spiritual direction group that is open to doing this work together, join us at the Presence Project to find groups of different sizes. You'd be surprised how beautiful this work can be shoulder to shoulder.

Part II Introduction to Attachment Practices

1. Dr. Karl Lehman of Immanuel Approach and Life Model Works has done exceptional work talking about how recalling joy-filled moments opens up our relational capacity and our ability to listen to God. Try their book, *The Joyful Journey*.

2. Beloved author Ann Voskamp has done a beautiful job explaining how our life can be changed by gratitude in her book *One Thousand Gifts*.

3. Marriage and family therapist Nicole Zasowski has developed a practice called savoring, which invites us to slowly connect to each sense within a memory. This gives joy a chance to root.

4. Therapist Deb Dana invites us to heal trauma by remembering glimmers, which are moments of joy in our everyday life.

Chapter 11 A Tangible Reminder

1. This was from a conversation between Richard Foster and his son, Nathan, at Trinity Anglican Westside in March 2017 during a book tour for Nathan's book, *The Making of an Ordinary Saint*.

2. *Our Modern Services of the Anglican Church of Kenya* (Frisco, Kenya: The Ekklesia Society, 2008), 84.

Chapter 12 Posture

1. Brother Lawrence, *Practice of the Presence: A Revolutionary Translation*, Cameron Acevedo Butcher, trans. (Minneapolis: Broadleaf Books, 2022), 14, 21.

2. Lawrence, *Practice of the Presence*, from Beaufort's Profile, 152–66.

3. Lawrence, *Practice of the Presence of God*, 31.

Chapter 13 Repentance

1. Most of this practical invitation to repent was taken from the Healing Care Group curriculum. To lead your small group or church in this transformative curriculum, find it here: https://www.healingcare.org/healing-care-group-curriculum.

2. "H7291—*radaph*," *Strong's Hebrew Lexicon (NIV)*, Blue Letter Bible, accessed October 12, 2023, https://www.blueletterbible.org/lexicon/h7291/niv/wlc/0-1/.

3. See John 8:1–11.

4. Lawrence, *Practice of the Presence of God*, 29.

5. Marilyn Vancil, *Beyond the Enneagram: An Invitation to Experience a More Centered Life with God* (New York: Crown Publishing Group, 2022), 19.

Chapter 14 Lectio Divina

1. Thelma Hall, monastic and author, has described the rest after Lectio Divina in this way: "There is an inner dynamic in the evolution of all true love that leads to a level of communication 'too deep for words.' There the lover becomes inarticulate, falls silent, and the beloved receives the silence as eloquence." *Too Deep for Words: Rediscovering Lectio Divina* (Mahwah, NJ: Paulist Press, 1988), 7.

2. Quoted in Leanne Payne, *Restoring the Christian Soul: Overcoming Barriers to Completion in Christ through Healing Prayer* (Grand Rapids: Baker, 1996), 2.

3. Macrina Wiederkehr, *A Tree Full of Angels: Seeing the Holy in the Ordinary* (San Francisco: HarperCollins, 2012), 26.

4. Philip Yancey, "The Death of Reading Is Threatening the Soul," *Washington Post*, July 21, 2017, https://www.washingtonpost.com/news/acts-of-faith/wp/2017/07/21/the-death-of-reading-is-threatening-the-soul/?utm_term=.f9edb488d831.

5. See Luke 24:13–35.

Chapter 15 The 3 R's

1. Terry Wardle, *Every Breath We Take: Living in the Presence, Love, and Generosity of God* (Abilene, TX: Leafwood Publishers, 2015).

2. This beautiful practice of asking God "Where are You in the room on my behalf?" was taught by Dr. Anne Halley as a way to begin learning that attachment love is always at hand.

Chapter 16 Breath Prayer

1. I heard a talk by Brendan Manning twenty years ago on a recording and began praying this prayer. I also know that he teaches this breath prayer in his book *The Furious Longing of God*.

Chapter 17 Silence

1. "The Importance of Cocooning," Gifts of Grace, accessed July 28, 2023, https://www.giftsofgraceadoption.com/cocooning/.

2. Michael J. Harter, *Hearts on Fire: Praying with* Jesuits (Chicago: Loyola Press, 2005), 7–8.

3. Henri J. M. Nouwen, *The Way of the Heart: Desert Spirituality and Contemporary Ministry* (New York: Seabury Press, 1981), 27.

4. Imke Kirste et al., "Is Silence Golden? Effects of Auditory Stimuli and Their Absence on Adult Hippocampal Neurogenesis," *Brain Structure and Function* 220, no. 2 (2015): 1221–28, https://www.ncbi.nlm.nih.gov/pmc/articles/PMC4087081/.

5. I now get to be associate faculty at the same spiritual direction certificate program I once took part in. If you like anything you've read in this book and you're interested in the work of spiritual direction, please check us out at https://www.healingcare.org/direction.

Chapter 18 Ignatian Imaginative Prayer

1. Corrie ten Boom, *The Hiding Place: An Engaging Visual Journey* (Bloomington, MN: Chosen, 2023), 207.

2. Gregory A. Boyd, *Seeing Is Believing: Experience Jesus Through Imaginative Prayer* (Grand Rapids: Baker Books, 2004), 90.

3. Quoted in Richard J. Foster, *Sanctuary of the Soul: Journey into Meditative Prayer* (Downers Grove, IL: InterVarsity Press, 2011), 37.

4. *An Experiment in Criticism* by CS Lewis © copyright 1961 CS Lewis Pte Ltd. Extract used with permission.

5. Ignatius of Loyola, *The Autobiography of St. Ignatius* (New York: Benziger Brothers, 1900).

6. Finding God in All Things: A Marquette Prayer Book. ©2009 Marquette University.

7. Richard J. Foster, *Prayer: Finding the Heart's True Home* (Hong Kong: HarperCollins, 1992), 147.

8. Richard J. Foster, *Celebration of Discipline: The Path to Spiritual Growth* (New York: HarperCollins, 1988), 19.

9. Transformation Intensive website, accessed July 28, 2023, https://transform ationintensive.org/.

10. J. M. Kilner and R. N. Lemon, "What We Know Currently about Mirror Neurons," *Current Biology* 2, no. 23 (December 2013): R1057–62, https://www.ncbi.nlm .nih.gov/pmc/articles/PMC3898692/.

11. Sourya Acharya and Samarth Shukla, "Mirror Neurons: Enigma of the Metaphysical Modular Brain," *Journal of Natural Science, Biology, and Medicine* 2, no. 3 (July 2012): 118–24, https://doi.org/10.4103/0976-9668.101878.

Chapter 19 Lament

1. Immanuel Journaling was developed by Sungshim Loppnow and Jim Wilder as a brilliant prayer exercise for us to experience God's attunement to our suffering. It's explained in the book *The Joyful Journey* and can be found here: https://lifemodel works.org/wp-content/uploads/2018/08/Joyful-Journey-Questions.pdf; E. James Wilder et al., *Joyful Journey: Listening to Immanuel* (East Peoria, IL: Shepherd's House, Inc., 2015).

2. Melissa F. Greene, "30 Years Ago Romania Deprived Thousands of Children of Human Contact: Here's What's Become of Them," *The Atlantic*, July 1, 2020, https:// doi.org/10/9/2023.

3. Jude Cassidy and Phillip R. Shaver, eds., *Handbook of Attachment: Theory, Research, and Clinical Applications* (New York: Guilford Publications, 2018), 267.

Conclusion

1. Luke 2:19: "But Mary treasured up all these things and pondered them in her heart."

2. "Flickering Mind," by Denise Levertov, from A DOOR IN THE HIVE, copyright ©1989 by Denise Levertov. Reprinted by permission of New Directions Publishing Corp.

3. Miklós Vetö, *The Religious Metaphysics of Simone Weil*, trans. Joan Dargan (New York: State University of New York Press, 1994), 45.

4. "Patient Trust," excerpted from Michael Harter, ed., *Hearts on Fire: Praying with Jesuits* (Chicago: Loyola Press, 2004), 102–3.

Meet the Author

Summer Joy Gross (MDiv, Virginia Theological Seminary) is an Anglican priest, retreat leader, and spiritual director whose work is guided by the belief that our stories can be transformed by God's invitation to make His love our home base. She is associate faculty with Spiritual Formation and the Art of Spiritual Direction at the Healing Care Ministries' spiritual direction school. She is the host of *The Presence Project Podcast* and lives in Georgia with her husband, their three teenagers, and their Brittany spaniel, who points out lawn ornament rabbits around their suburban neighborhood.

Connect with Summer:

SummerJoyGross.com

@SummerGross

@RevSummerJoy

Rev. Summer Joy Gross

Patreon.com/ThePresenceProject